100

A Journey of Discovery: On Writing for Children

Books by Ivan Southall

MACMILLAN PUBLISHING CO., INC.
Josh
Head in the Clouds
Benson Boy
Matt and Jo
Hills End
Seventeen Seconds
Fly West
A Journey of Discovery

ST. MARTIN'S PRESS, INC.
Ash Road
The Curse of Cain
Let the Balloon Go
Sly Old Wardrobe (with Ted Greenwood)
Finn's Folly
Chinaman's Reef Is Ours

BRADBURY PRESS, INC.
Walk a Mile and Get Nowhere

A Journey of Discovery:

On Writing for Children

Ivan Southall

Macmillan Publishing Co., Inc.
New York

Macmillan Publishing Co., Inc., 866 Third Avenue, New York, N.Y. 10022
Collier Macmillan Canada, Ltd.
First American edition, 1976
Printed in the United States of America
1 2 3 4 5 6 7 8 9 10

Library of Congress Cataloging in Publication Data
Southall, Ivan.
    A journey of discovery.

    1. Southall, Ivan.   2.   Children's literature—
History and criticism—Addresses, essays, lectures.
I. Title.
PR9619.3.S6Z514   1976   809'.89282   75–31547
ISBN 0–02–786150–3

Contents

A Journey of Discovery: On Writing for Children

Note

It is a tradition, and a bad one I am told, to begin a serious work with an apology. And this is a very serious work. And a very serious apology. This book sets out to tell you how I go about writing books for children, and that is a *terribly* serious matter, believe me. The world is full of experts busy proving it, but I am not expert at proving anything.

Despite its brevity, it is a work put together over a long period, a collection of opinions and reflections around a central theme that I have expressed on paper or on the public platform during the course of several years. Once, no one would have wasted time listening to me, and after today I hope no one will need to. Everything the man wants to say for the present about his craft is here; it is said; it is done.

Kindly note the operative end of the title, *On Writing for Children*. Four words, not three. So this is not a handbook or a manual or a treatise on how to do anything. It will not turn a row-boat into a yacht, or a reader into a writer, or a rank amateur into a polished professional, but something is here, and I have spent the last three years travelling to the ends of the earth to say it.

An enormous emotional effort has gone into the preparation and delivery of these lectures and into the life out of which they have come, a life not lived asleep underneath a hat. The lectures have been revised and rewritten dozens of times, and spoken, in one form or another, perhaps hundreds of times. They go on developing, thought by thought, out of my search for literary and self-understanding and are very much a personal statement. There might not be another writer working for children who agrees with me.

The lectures have come together in this book because I wanted to see them together, because there were things I wished to say permanently, because I felt there should be an accessible place where my point of view was available.

The whole thing probably ends up being a philosophy, not as from a philosopher, but from a simple man who is not one-half as complicated as his critics sometimes assert, or as sinister either.

1 Journeys of Discovery

First published in the Children's Book and
Educational Supplement, *Australian Book Review*,
July 1969. It was an answer to a question from the
editor of the journal – "When is a children's book
not a children's book?" No alteration to any
original viewpoint has been made in this expanded
statement.

"Know thyself", as a rule to live by, is said to be a critical
factor in the rounded development of a human being, but I am
not certain that the writer is wise who subjects his attitudes and
work to over-frequent self-examination, whether he does it
gladly or is moved by a sense of duty to satisfy his questioners.
Hence, I wonder whether this exercise is an act of folly. I
wonder whether I shall come to regret it?

Each book, I am already sure, should be its own statement
without prologues or epilogues from the author, and I shall go
on expressing this belief. It is one of the few things in writing I
have no doubt about. People who seek explanations of this
kind from a writer – what is the origin of a certain book or
character or situation *and why* – may personally be moved by
the best of motives, but may place the writer in a corner if he
has not reached a confident maturity. If the writer learns too
much too soon about his own processes, from himself or from
others, he may impose controls to revise or correct patterns or
idiosyncrasies that could be his assets. It does not follow that a
source of *irritation* to a given reader is a weakness in the make-up
of the writer. There is an equal risk that the writer may attach
importance to himself and start striking attitudes and postures
he does not genuinely feel. He may start believing his own

9

publicity sheets – tailored to the specifications required by commerce!

These feelings deepened as month by month my encounters with editors, writers and critics multiplied. This odd situation began to arise after a long obscurity when I discovered, with surprise, that serious readers were taking me seriously. It was an odd experience; in a fashionable term, *traumatic*. "Are they *really* talking about me? Is there not a confusion somewhere? If that's what they think about *my* books, what sort of rubbish is everybody else writing?" Literally, you pinch yourself, and it hurts, and you're alive, and a nervousness grows, a vulnerability grows.

Now I find that academic questions aimed at drawing me out, for any reason, are becoming almost too dangerous to answer. They involve me in days of conflict and assessment I would rather give to new writing, and sometimes I wonder whether this is why I am beginning to argue impatiently, even testily, as I hear what I am saying. Am I already striking postures despite my awareness of the risk?

Is this fellow Southall, people ask, really a writer for children? Does it matter a damn when scores of thousands of children reading in about twenty languages suggest that the question is pointless?

It seems to me that the deeper the chord a writer chances to strike, the wilder are the assertions his adult critics make. Children participate in another dimension. So I know of the disturbed and sensitive child who reads six times to his benefit the story many adults deplore as terrifying – *The Fox Hole*. And, about the same book, I hear of the third graders, several years running, who live wholesomely through the same experience because a teacher understands it, and year after year from her class come drawings and letters and kisses to my home. And from another adult I hear of the handicapped boy who sleeps with *Let the Balloon Go*, who wears out copy after copy, who charts his boyhood by it. The experts said: "What harm this will do; keep it out of the reach of the handicapped."

Sometimes I am confused about where I stand, sometimes I do not know what I really think – particularly under pressure from a live audience – and can be guilty of foolish ambiguities, but at this moment I see my function clearly. I *do* write books for children, consciously so, to entertain and involve and extend them, and for every adult who urges me out of his wisdom to reassess my position, there is someone who says, "Take no notice. Don't stop. Keep going." It is good to hear it from anyone; it is wonderful to hear it from children. It is odd that children get to know, come to hear of it. "You're not writing for them, Mr Southall. You're writing for us. Why care what they say?"

Approaching the question, "when is a children's book not a children's book?" I immediately suggest that the clause assumes attitudes imposed by widely-accepted terms based upon standards or judgements that may not be supportable or acceptable, and that have been responsible for misrepresenting the function of writers of serious intention. These terms, "children's book", "juvenile", and others like them, are convenient for the purpose of cataloguing and criticism and displaying on counters, but the writer should not be intimidated by them. If the writer is not honest with himself, if he is too much concerned with limitations imposed upon him from the outside in the form of commercial or academic definitions, his creativity is stifled, the so-called "mirror" he holds up to life whether in fantasy or realism is distorted, and the integrity he thought he had turns out to be a disposable commodity.

"Juvenile" is a term that has irritated me always, even when the best book I could write for children was an inferior one. It is a most unfortunate term because of its connotations and how it gained acceptance and continues in usage, *even on publishers' lists*, is completely beyond me. Every time I see it something clicks in me; it is destructive; it provokes and promotes and generates its own silliness. How much rubbish has it been responsible for, directly and indirectly? How many good writers has it turned away from children? How many opportunists has it sucked in? Upon how many unfortunate kids has it inflicted drayloads of inanities?

"Children's book" is a sweeping generalization, like cake or woollen garment, denoting to the innocent adult (simply from usage) that a given volume may be left to Junior with no danger of awkward questions afterwards, no fear of emotional tensions or social backlash, and no risk of advancing the troublesome business of his maturation which will "sort of happen" anyway, everyone hopes, as long as everyone ignores it. It is assumed that in a "children's book" all will be violets and roses or uncomplicated swashbuckling adventure involving nothing other than an elementary chain of incident. Sweetness and light. Happiness ever after. Or wholesome and hearty bloodlust and thunder.

Of course, there is a place for the elementary, of course there is a place for violets and roses, but writing for children is seen by so many as the ultimate form of escapism – as an escape from the hard world into an incredible realm of utter impossibilities and abject absurdities where no critical standards need apply, where everything is scaled down, where nothing is man-size, where low-key left-handed exercises abound and creative integrity is over-ruled by expediency or mid-Victorian morality, and the classics are unassailable. Realism – in the sense of *reality* – is believed to be unattainable or undesirable; ideas, abstracts and social issues are unacceptable, and the serious craftsman must prostitute his talents or give them a holiday and the major writer would never be found at all unless he lived a very long time ago.

These standards linger in surprising places. Minds remain anchored to traditional patterns that never had the virtue of logic or the dignity of childhood. Very sloppy conceptions they are, limiting content and imposing restrictions on theme, depth, and even physical dimensions – things like the number of words in a story and the number of pages in a book – as if children were standardized, mass-produced vessels into which measured doses of syrup can be poured. And if you consistently feed short-winded concepts to children – or to anyone – they become accepted as the total, and departures from the pattern are received with fear or incomprehension.

Yet how can honest kids relate to the traditional characters of fiction written for them, or films made for them, or entertainment devised for them? The kids say "thanks" to please you and cheer to be in the swim. If ever the inanities inflicted upon them by the media each day give them time to reflect, *what on earth do the children think?* How can children fit the traditional pattern of reading and entertainment into the reality of the lives they live? In *Let the Balloon Go*, John Clement Sumner, the spastic boy, cries, "Do they think I'm a bunch of flowers?"

I would like to think that John speaks for children. I would like to think that boys and girls recognize themselves in him. I would like to think that parents recognize themselves also, and see that the restrictions John cries against are symbolic of the barriers and prohibitions dedicated unwittingly, even with pure love and affection, to the raising of morons and misfits. Ill-adjusted people are by no means a modern invention, even if the techniques for producing them are constantly subject to improvement.

Of books, conscience is a vital component; the power of the word is terrifying and the flight of a single thought is unpredictable. When a writer creates books that are given to children his responsibility for truth to the limits of his vision is inescapable. If I consider my responsibility to its ultimate measurement I am tempted to knock off writing altogether, but I don't; I buckle my belt and anoint my head and march on hoping for the wisdom to avoid serious error.

The writer must weigh his choices in a critical balance, thus exercising his freedom as well as his function. There are times when he will need courage as he strives for absolute honesty: does he face life for his readers and set precedents for their future experience, or does he manipulate incident and character to spare himself the inconvenience of criticism? As I see it, the only choice the writer has is to face life as his own experience has revealed it, even if the discovery of a lie in a completed manuscript forces extensive revision or reworking. This happened to me with *Bread and Honey*. Accepted by my publishers, almost prepared for printing, I recalled it and entirely rewrote it, with my editor's encouragement. This was the story of a boy's emotional awakening and I had been afraid to face the sexuality of it. The Michael in my heart was not the Michael on paper. For six months young Michael Cameron kept me awake, Michael and every other boy who should have been able to see himself in one part or another of Michael's dilemma. I called for Michael and he came home again to spend another six months with me. So here and there librarians ban him.

In comparatively recent years, children's books, as a generalization, have been dragged up from a trough of superficiality and mediocrity and set in higher places. This drive towards creative excellence for children is an exciting advance of twentieth-century literature, but having started it are some of its originators and prophets and disciples afraid of its destination? Or are we hearing the clankings of the "old guard" ghost that resides in the heart of each of us?

In my own professional life the need for something better, for a more *productive* role, led me towards a revision of fundamental attitudes and to a degree of fulfilment not only outside the bounds of my capacity as I saw it, but into a kind of wonderland. This fulfilment was based on my earlier awakening – apparent in *Hills End* which I wrote in 1960 - to the simple truth that real adventure is not in heroic incident or heroic character, but in the lives of ordinary people. It needed world-wide recognition of *Hills End* to convince me I was not mistaken. Almost six years lie between the conception of that book and the next expression of what it started for me.

Ash Road was a long time in coming and for this the reason was simple enough. In Australia – where the reaction to my work is the *most* important to me – *Hills End*, with a few warm exceptions, was received with coolness and self-righteous pomposity.

14

Hills End, it was said, was not a proper book to give to children. Its ideas, its terror, its "power", its adult logic and its denouement were unacceptable or harmful. It "fell between two stools" – whatever that was supposed to mean. It was neither a book for children nor a book for adults, but simply a writer's self-indulgence. I was then too thin-skinned and underconfident and insecure to take that kind of discouragement, which I read as a personal attack on me.

Initially, *Hills End* was rejected even by my publishers with the comment that it was worth reconstruction. I imagine this was a gentle way of saying it was not worth anything. But Beatrice Davis of Angus & Robertson had second thoughts; she reversed the unanimous decision of her readers that the book was a failure and convinced the Publication Committee to issue it, but two years were to elapse before she was able to get it between covers. Subsequently, the distribution of this book in numerous and on-going editions and in many languages and hundreds of thousands of copies would seem to indicate that children can cope with it. Now there are critics who ask, "Where has the mood gone? Why can't he recapture it?" Revealing not only the shortness of their memories but their ignorance of what a writer is about.

I would suggest on the evidence of the first few years of criticism, both hostile and laudatory, of this author only, as a serious writer for children, that the question posed in this essay should be viewed with suspicion.

He is a rash man who declares or defines the fence beyond which a book of honest intention is to have the distinction of "children's reading" stripped from it.

The term "children", like "children's book", is a generalization. The encounter is with the child. The child may skate across its surface, he may live it in substance, he may put the book down. He will make his own decision as an individual. Let the adult say if he will, "This is unsuitable; this will disturb; this will perplex; this will harm", that is his personal privilege of opinion, but let him know that his risk of error is as great as the author's.

A child lives in the world, not on a pedestal. He is out among people, not under glass.

It might be obvious, it might be rhetorical, to point out that a child dirties his hands, that he loves and hates, that he is weak and strong, but these are the things I weigh when I choose the theme that will fill my life for an indefinite period. I have written in a month a book I proudly own, I have written others in a year; time is not important once the choice is made. The theme must be dredged, not feared or manipulated. It is a journey of discovery with decisions in every line. Involvement, not innovation, is the guide to the validity of these decisions rather than academic assessment of right or wrong, then or later. Involvement is the whole person, head and heart, and what today cannot solve tomorrow will reveal. You cannot manufacture legitimate incident any more than you can manufacture the sure judgement of hindsight; you must wait on discovery. The more difficult the theme the more exciting the journey and from what themes of life are living children excluded?

Plot is an irrationality. Who can plot tomorrow?

2 To Build a Book

On 21 May 1971, the author delivered a lecture to
the School of Librarianship, University of New
South Wales, during the course of a seminar on
Australian books for children. Variations on the
original lecture were read before the Children's
Book Council of Queensland; at the University of
California, Berkeley; at the University of Exeter
in England; and for the National Book Development
Council of Singapore.

The following version contains additional
material drawn from an article published in the
*Journal of the School Library Association of North
Queensland*, September 1968.

Something has been happening to children; I am sure you must
have noticed. There are more of them around than there used
to be. More than half the human race now. We are being overwhelmed by them. The human race is in danger of being
outnumbered by itself.

Something has happened to man. He is maturing earlier. In
an intellectual and in an emotional sense, by the time he is
twelve or thirteen or fourteen, he seems to be two or three years
ahead of what he used to be. Not of what he used to be a thousand years ago, or a century ago, but apparently of what he
used to be a generation ago. Kids have staged a revolution.
Look at what kids have done to this world in the last few years.
Treated it as if they owned it, while the grey-beards have
wagged their fingers and clicked their tongues and ordered out
the home guard with machine-guns.

When we talk of children these are the people we are thinking
of. And when we speak of their books, of the books being written

for them now, we speak of a kind of book we did not have when we were children ourselves. We would not have been able to read it. I doubt if we would have been able to understand it.

The development of the serious novel for children would appear to have been a spontaneous growth simultaneously in many parts of the world. I am not a student of literature in a historical sense, so I cannot tell you how this development came about or out of which sources it sprang, or, indeed, whether there are genuine relationships other than in the most general terms of form. It is likely that many writers share my feelings. We are too busy writing to worry about the "why" of it, and probably many of us are unfamiliar with the work of our contemporaries, however regrettable observers might consider this to be.

The only books I have read seriously in recent years are works of adult non-fiction for the purpose of review. The only books for children I have read since childhood are my own and then only in the course of writing them. Not at any time have I returned to read one of my books as a book. Yet I share with most writers the conviction that books are my life. I work in the midst of them. I have a private library of perhaps two and a half thousand volumes. They influence me by their presence, by their auras, and I long to know them better, but when I put down my pen there is little left except fatigue. My recreation is sleep or physical exercise. I could count on the fingers of one hand the occasions when ideas of value have come to me away from my desk. The desk and the pen are the keys.

I live in a community. Hence I am a chairman of things and a secretary of things, and every day, in one or another way, I am drawn into the affairs of the community, and not infrequently for several whole days in succession. Herein lies a problem shared by all writers whose names are known not only locally, but beyond the bottoms of their own streets.

Precisely where does the obligation of the writer lie? Is it to people through the book or is it to people face to face? Do the innumerable well-meaning people who ask him to write a little piece for their club newsletter as an act of friendship, or to speak for an hour off the cuff to their group, whatever that group may be, ever consider or care that someone else might have asked yesterday and someone else will ask tomorrow and the author, if he said *yes* to all, would positively never have time to function creatively?

I am convinced more of the folly than the wisdom of occupying a stage, even though I go on doing it. It exhausts the nervous energy and places the writer in a position where he is compelled to talk about himself, even to the point of embarrassment, because honesty must be the rule or the exercise is pointless. And in how many different ways can one individual relate a few simple and relevant facts about himself and his work without boring himself stupid? Or, perhaps, without occasionally in the recklessness or impatience of the moment lapsing into excess? Even when he mocks himself (as he must often do if he is not to inflate his own importance), even when he jokes pointedly at his own expense, there are members of every audience who take him seriously and leave him standing there, pale or flushed, regretting himself.

From another viewpoint: in what possible way can he or should he illuminate the meaning of an existing book to an audience? Simply as a committed writer he asks every relevant question of himself during the process of forming the book, and once it is formed the problem belongs to the reader. The book itself must be the answer to all questions about itself and must stand without additional propping up.

The author on the public platform may find himself assailed by unanswerable questions, perhaps relating to an issue of development in a book written five or six or ten years ago, something he hasn't looked at or thought of since. He is reluctant to name the characters, admitting the possibility of naming them from the wrong book, and what a fool he would look then. Yet this takes nothing from the sincerity of the original act of writing, but half a million words or more demanding the same sincerity and the same involvement have crowded through his life during the intervening years. Dare he really stand on a public stage, swimming at the shore of a sea of faces, his mouth wide open and say, "Did I write that?"

The problem is not without point. His doubts could be genuinely based. He *is* going to be asked questions about books he did not write. And sooner or later he will be introduced to an audience by a beaming chairman as the script writer of a television series he has never heard of. And I ask you, how do you get out of that kind of situation without hurting people? Or, if the writer is a simple soul educated to the eighth-and-a-half grade, he can encounter words entirely beyond his experience. Can a writer really say, "I'm sorry. You'll have to ask me again. In easier words than that." It has happened to me, though once or twice I have bluffed it through, *I think!* Or from the younger generation he is likely to encounter – and cross my heart, this is the genuine stuff:

"Are you a millionaire, Mister?"

"I reckon you'd be a terrific father, or do you belt them about?"

"Did you write *The ABZ of Love*?" – this from a Primary School fifth grader in the deepest depths of rural Victoria, aged ten! Write it? I haven't even read it. I'm not allowed to yet.

I am seriously of the opinion that any challenge to the statement which is the substance of a book should be ignored by the writer. Fights should be fought out between the writer's critics and his champions, preferably behind his back and without his knowledge of it. The author who endeavours to justify himself, particularly in print, does so at his own peril, until he is BIG enough to be unassailable. The ordinary, life-size author should accept that he cannot win – and he must be a person of raw sensitivity or he would not be a creative writer. If, in specific reply to printed criticism, he goes into print himself he is only going to be hurt further. I wince every time I observe an outraged writer attempt to reply to written criticism of himself or his book, and I could weep for him if he initiates legal proceedings.

The writer hears an extraordinary amount of drivel about his books perpetrated in the name of review or criticism.* There are critics and critics, *of course*, just as there are books and books, and I am not meaning to implant the idea that I am in a state of constant murderous intent when contemplating people who review my work. Well, I don't think I am. There was a time when I seriously considered the comments of certain critics and for a while I believed they had helped constructively to modify some of my less desirable tendencies. I no longer hold this opinion; to heed them was a mistake; they tripped me and contributed to my loss of confidence in my direction as a writer. I no longer read them. The writer must follow his own star. Criticism is for others to read, for their amusement or guidance or instruction. Not for the writer.

But criticism "looms large" in the life of the writer. Even though he may draw away from its sources, the stream rushes on; others remain involved and the writer is drawn into their discussions and arguments; clippings arrive on his desk although he might have cancelled his subscriptions; the telephone rings with a breathless report of some fresh excess; a friend stops him in the street; a letter comes in the post; a member of an audience frames a question. There is never a total escape from it.

Most mature writers can take mature criticism, I should stress that, but there are sources of criticism that provoke us to pain or anger or laughter. There will come words that are unquestionably libellous, that few people not in a writer's position would tolerate, and you find yourself unhappily awake at night. I doubt if there is a serious writer anywhere who has not had to live with this form of spiritual assault. If he is a writer for children he is likely to endure it with tiresome regularity.

How often have I seen bigoted or addle-headed reviewers

* Thoughts on critics and criticism differ substantially from those held in 1969, the time of first writing. Much of the original material has been deleted or modified.

attack the theme of a book by manipulating the theme to provide the basis of their moral attack against it, and this can be a remarkable feat of gymnastics, verbally and ethically. Then in Australia, notably one could say, there flourishes another kind of sport, riding the Great Australian Hobby Horse, our inferiority complex, which goes down to history very slowly, though everyone professes the desire to be rid of it. When there is nothing else to say and the cut of the author's cloth irritates, they tell him he pinches his plot, whatever that may be, from some other fellow, usually American or English-born. This is the very bottom of the critic's barrel of goodies: in print, declaring the obligation of a fellow-countryman to an overseas influence for themes and services rendered – not because he has the reputation for stealing the property of other writers, but *because* he is a fellow-countryman. This is to infer that an Australian, by nature, is incapable of thinking or feeling for himself and cannot possibly take offence no matter how vigorously you defame him. One author I know used to go outside to slash about a ton of firewood into chips to cool off, while his wife leapt into the car and rushed off to visit friends.

It is probably not necessary to repeat that I am speaking of the novel for children, although many of the tribulations under review do come to the writers of novels for adults. Not *all*, however, because it is known that novels for adults are written by human beings who might occasionally, from elementary human weakness, propagate slightly questionable principles. But the writer for children comes under a different form of scrutiny and sooner or later they'll get him for something, even if it's for sucking his soup and setting a bad example. Along with the unfortunate parson, who has to file his humanity in the archives, the writer for children cannot be flesh and blood except at the risk of incurring the judgements of the self-righteous.

While he writes his poor but honest rubbish, while his spirit grows and his craftsmanship matures, the world virtually ignores him, he has time for a private life, hardly any professional cares and almost no responsibilities. On a good day he might dare to wink at a pleasing person of the opposite gender, without first having been introduced, and to hell with the consequences. He might come home drunk or shout at his wife or gambol unclothed amongst the buttercups, and no one will bat an eyelid – writers, after all, are known to be colourful characters. Of course he might starve because the libraries won't buy him, but it is common knowledge that writers are used to privation, and if you place him downwind of the local fish and chip shop, with instructions to breathe deeply night and morning, you may confidently expect him to survive indefinitely. At least, until he grows up and starts writing with a shade of significance. Beyond that day his survival may well depend upon how thick his skin is, unless he is prepared to return to sources. In this sense he is fortunate.

The writer for children should communicate with children regularly, children other than those who live beside him. He should visit a school certainly once or twice a month to *feel* children around him, and he should be prepared to travel distances – in essential things the children beyond the horizon may be the same as the children in the next room, but there are differences of opportunity and environment and development that can add significantly to the writer's experience. Out of that experience his work may become more relevant.

He should answer every reader's letter that he receives. As far as I know every boy or girl who has written to me has had a letter, usually handwritten, back again. But on my desk, within reach of my outstretched arm, is a thin manilla folder with a few letters inside: one that says, "You will answer me, won't you, because they say you won't." But Ben has not had his answer. I have no idea where Ben lives. Sometimes letters arrive in German or Japanese or other languages outside my ken. Translation can be difficult. Consulates are not always helpful; I am not an industrialist. There are moments of crisis brought about by bright-eyed young school teachers whose silver tongues may one day get them into real trouble. Huge parcels arrive on my desk – one a tube four inches in diameter and thirty inches long –

packed with letters. Dozens and dozens of letters and stories and questions and valentines in a single post for which one eager beaver junior teacher will be responsible. For some of these a form of composite letter has been arranged! For others no composite letter could possibly fit. There was no such escape from a teacher's request for forty photographs measuring six inches by four to be awarded as prizes. I have often wondered what her kids thought of their prizes. Nor can there be stock answers to love letters, from teenage girls dreaming, beautiful letters I will always remember. Perhaps I should spell it out – there can be stock answers to nothing. I think of a petition from a tiny country school way out in the far west signed by everybody from Grade One up:

Dear Mr Southall,
   To The Wild Sky is an interesting book. [Not brilliant, kindly note, just interesting.] Half of us reckon they die. Half of us don't. Helen says they get married and have kids. Sir says if you're going to write a sequel will you hurry up. We like Mark because he's a pest.

A few times, instead of my going to schools, schools have driven out to meet me at my home in the bush. Kids getting out of buses and swarming from the road up the hill. It's a sight a writer is not likely to forget. A garden full of kids; flowers and trees and kids. A house full of kids all sitting on the floor. You talk to each other for a while. Forty-three want to use the lavatory – and we're on rainwater tanks with two-quart septic sewerage. In groups of half-a-dozen they'll come on into the study, faces like a school photograph filling the door.
   "Gee, d'you write 'em there?"
   "Is that your wife when she was a girl? Pretty, *wasn't* she?"
   "What's that up there? Is that an emu egg up there? Whatchoo got an emu egg for? Hey, look, he's got an emu egg up there."
   "Whatcha got a wash basin in the corner for?"
   "Can I sit in your chair? Can I swing it around? He sits here, you know. This is where he does it."

"Is that the aeroplane you flew?"

"Can I plug in your razor and have a shave?"

"I didn't sleep all night, Mr Southall. It was such a long night waiting to come here to see you."

Or perhaps at a High School in an industrial area ("Culturally deprived kids," the teacher had said, framing her invitation, "they did not believe it when I said you might come.") – where you have spoken to audiences of junior form students since 9 a.m. and signed hundreds of autographs and paused not once, you'll walk wearily to your car at about 3.45 p.m. and want to die. Hoarse and headachy and stupefied and a forty-five mile drive home and someone will tap on the window glass and you'll wind it down. A fifth former or a sixth former, a young man looking sheepish, with a worn copy of *Hills End* in his hand: "Mr Southall, would you sign it for me, please?"

Or you struggle with a manuscript for five months and it will not *go*, it will not come alive, in five cheerless months you have seventy-two pages as dead as the dodo, yet something "in your bones" will not allow you to wrap it up and climb the ladder to the ceiling and commit it to the burial cupboard where the dead manuscripts lie, those numerous books that refused to form. The telephone rings day after day; does it ever stop? The things you're chairman of and secretary of generate crises every twenty-four hours. Elizabeth is terrified by a dog half as big as a horse and you run a hundred and fifty yards to bring her home across the road. A tradesman calls in to fix something and for two hours talks beside the heater duct filling the house with his noise. A religious group is at the door, hiding behind a small child, and will not go away. A fellow on a property nearby, bless his heart and soul, starts up his chain saw. There are a dozen impatient letters in the post demanding answers every day. It rains and rains and rains and you're cold. And every frustrated day is the same as the frustrated day that went before. And your wife says, "Put it all in the car and go away."

"I can't put it in the car." And your voice breaks and turns thin. "How can I? I've never gone away. I've always managed at home. And what's the use of going away? A week won't do. A month won't do. I don't know how long it will take. I don't know."

"Put it in the car and go away."

So you cancel everything, and that's not easy, and put it in the car, all of it, and you go, and for the only time in your professional life you write an entire book on your own. At peace.

Every second weekend the family comes to see you as if visiting you in prison. Indeed, they take home the car. No telephone. No mail. No radio or TV. And the nearest newspaper shop is a walk around of four miles. The corner shop with the public telephone for ringing home is about three-quarters of a mile. So every morning at about 9.30 you head off along the beach to the corner shop to buy your odds and ends for the day, your feet breaking virgin sand and the world belongs to you. For two and a half months you live like a beachcomber, working well and eating well and sleeping well, in the best health you have enjoyed in years, lying naked and content in the sun for an hour each afternoon (tanned, never before, never since), yet disciplined, and except for the family no one ever coming to the door.

Twelve, thirteen, fourteen hours, working at it every day, working aloud, acting and speaking the story as it unfolds, vividly reliving the wonder of being the boy that you were long ago, with a dozen different falsettos for a dozen different characters, no one outside the window to overhear, no one in the next room to inhibit you, no one anywhere around to bottle you up or make you consciously aware that you are a man almost fifty years old. For eleven weeks all the defences and sobrieties of the years are put aside.

Can it ever happen again in quite the same way? Already I know it cannot come back; it belonged to then, to there, and the time; yet to return and sit in that window in the sun for an hour feelings begin to stir. It is strange. Move the desk to another place and it has gone. Magic is there, but only in a few square feet. I try to bring it back, but the shape of life changes;

I cannot get there again, alone, long enough for the key to turn. Perhaps I am meant to accept my seventy-seven days as a reward for other disciplines. Account paid in full, as it were. So I cut the tie. It has gone.

At the end of my seventy-seven days I held in my hand a constant surprise, the book I had not been able to find before, had never been able to unlock because someone or something always stood in the way. Even the seventy-two pages I started with, even they had been in the way. Not one of those pages survived.

I suppose *Josh* was the book I had written for myself, that I felt then could, and probably would, leave the rest of the world unmoved or confused, yet I believed it to be the only book I had written that was totally enclosed inside a shell of calm resistance to anything anyone could say about it. I was sure it had been written for an audience of one and that the audience had grown to be satisfied.

"If anyone else wants to read it when it's around," I said at the time, "they are welcome to do so, particularly any boy or girl of any age, and if it fails to please and you say so, I promise not to rant or storm or rush outside to the woodheap with an axe in my hand."

I broke that promise. *Josh* was not inside a shell. *Josh* was more naked than the others.

Where does the obligation of the writer lie? To whom is he ultimately responsible?

It is an obvious remark that not everyone can write for children or would want to. There are legions of writers who look upon kids' stuff as just about the very end of the road, the very bottom of the pit, the final prostitution of a talent that cannot make the grade in an adult world. Yes, I have had this said to me, and to such a person there is no reply. They know all the answers before they start, and one of these days I may be provoked to a reasoned reply. I have been much moved by the saying of Christ that associates the Kingdom of God with childhood and children. Many interpretations may be placed upon it, hence we have nine thousand and two variations of faith and ten thousand and two denominations, but among other things I like to regard the Kingdom of God as a state of mind, a state of awareness, a capacity to be enthralled by the quality of life here and now, and unless we are prepared to strive to regain a child-like sensitivity to spiritual and sensual experience, the simple wonder of being alive will not be for you or for me.

I find myself remembering the years, and the labour of those years, during which I produced three-quarters of a million words of fact or conjecture upon fact in books for adult readers. In general terms these books succeeded. None was disgraced critically and all earned reasonable royalties. Some are still available in corners here and there. The writing particularly of *Softly Tread the Brave*, a long time ago, was something like an exciting journey in a strange country; of all my books for adults the experience I am least likely to forget; yet it is not a large thing beside the experience of writing several of my books for children. These have been experiences in a different dimension, in which I have glimpsed for extended periods something of the state of mind that people have sought to induce by other means throughout much of man's history, in which I have learnt about subtleties of truth and honesty that in works allegedly of fact had entirely eluded me, or possibly in self-defence I had shied away from. The search for honesty is a rough journey and a surprising one. You may become frightened of it yourself when you find it, and there are others who will not tolerate it at close quarters and will call it by every opposite term they can put pen or tongue to. I do not necessarily blame them.

Do not mistake me : I am not endeavouring by self-aggrandize-ment to add stature to stories or books that have numerous imperfections and may be forgotten in a few years, but I am heading towards the only reason I know for their existence at the present time. The reason and the eventual justification and the continuing spur. Notably, *Hills End, Let the Balloon Go,* and *Bread and Honey* added to my life a joy that renewed faith in all kinds of things though they may not have anything like that effect upon adults who might read them. Yet, apart from the short chapter in *Let the Balloon Go* where John Clement Summer, the spastic boy, sings his victory song in the tree, the sustained pinnacle for me came in another book, in *Josh*, the book I have been telling you about. If there is a reply to the sophisticates who regard the writing of books for children as unmanly, as weak, or as evidence of a prostituted talent, perhaps it is the emotion you might feel in the middle of a still night as you lie awake and there are no thoughts forming except sleeping people breathing and frogs outside and all is well.

The act of writing and revelling in the making of a book for children to read is a complicated state of mind, in which the technical accomplishments of the adult permit you to play tricks with time and convert the result into words that function on a very subtle wavelength. There is some limitation of vocabulary in the academic sense, but I have yet to encounter difficulties that significantly delayed me. I believe it is possible to depict or portray virtually anything in words regularly used by us all. This does not mean that long words are out; we all enjoy occasionally the use of long or unfamiliar words, particularly those that tease us by their shape and sound.

One thing you will find in good books for children is the imaginative use of an everyday vocabulary without the slightest trace of writing down. It seems to be *impossible* for some writers to achieve. The attitude or state of mind that *will* produce this kind of writing, as far as I am concerned, is to be found in segments of my childhood which I am able to relive and stretch almost indefinitely. Not the things I did as a child – well, not necessarily – but the things I thought as a child and particularly the way I went about thinking them, the struggle towards an identity which I felt keenly, the acute response I had to experiences of the senses, the anxiety and trembling excitement of the great moments, the elation of the emotional tree-tops, the despair of pain and fear and failure, and the constant shadow of over-riding adult domination. I see nothing beneath the dignity of an adult in reliving any of them. To put away *childish* things is a disaster.

The serious writer simply has to mature before he is equipped to write well for children. There are exceptions, but few writers can recapture with fidelity and compassion the subtlety, the vigour, and the anguish of youth until they have left the experience, in relation to their own lives, a reasonable distance behind. I say this despite the disturbing gulf that seems to lie between the generations.

The young person wishes to be an adult and longs for adult experience, and takes it, more often than not, before he is able to understand it or control it. So, too, the young writer usually exercises his art or craft on what he believes to be adult themes, the more "adult" the better. Books for children belong to his past, to his childhood, and there they can stay. If this were not so the best children's books would be written by children, out of the heart of the childhood experience. However, this the child cannot do. He lives in a world of raw emotion, of excruciating extremes, but lacks the capacity and the wisdom to express at length its significance. He may crystallize moments in poems of rare beauty, but the fabric of the whole is a full-time occupation; he is too close for detachment, too involved minute by minute for sustained analysis, simply too busy living in the middle of it. When he does write a book, as he sometimes does, for the heck of it, or because the family believes he is Shakespeare reincarnated (Aunt Hesta looking thoughtful), it is usually a tale of unlikely adventure and dimly seen characters written faster and faster until it explodes in an implausibly happy ending, with the villain crushed beneath a roadroller, disembowelled by a bull, or burnt at the stake by savages. This, in his parents' opinion, and sometimes calamitously in the opinion of a teacher, is thoroughly publishable, every bit as good as the epics on television (it might be), and certainly as impressive as Biggles. Usually it has little or nothing to do with the real world around him, not because he is unaware of that world, but because he cannot *handle* it.

The body of the book I make for children is made up of pieces of me as a child, often imperfectly realized because years and adult experience and the grown-up compulsion to correct or reprove stand in the way. Yet the mark of my own children and of the children of my friends is stamped upon many characters. Then there are times when my awareness is clouded and from the surfaces of the clouds come mistakes. But sometimes I break through into a primordial place of startling but familiar colour, conflict and intensity, and find the words to match it in a vocabulary that belongs to the experience. Even then, often, I spoil it; the man gets in the way; the adult in me refuses to be sufficiently subdued and throws up an emotional block. Nevertheless, whether you win or lose as a writer, the struggle to see into the mind of the child that you were is an intellectual adventure far more rewarding and – from my point of view – far more inviting at the present time than other forms of literary experiment.

Perhaps it is the intensity of this approach that lies at the root of critical observations that in some of my books hysteria runs a whisker below the surface, principally in *The Fox Hole* and *Finn's Folly* and to a different degree in *Chinaman's Reef is Ours*. I cannot say that I agree or disagree – I don't know. Where matters of opinion are concerned I strive not to be dogmatic; I apply this rule as a reviewer when I fulfil that function, and I am equally reluctant to thump the tub about my own books. My opinion of my work changes, usually from the wildest enthusiasm at one point or another to the deepest and most desperate gloom. There are glorious hours when I am drunk with my brilliance and in numerous voices and in numerous ways (Cockney, County, BBC, Yankee, and Mediterranean Migrant) will read aloud again and again a few sublime pages. Absolutely nuts. Then there are days or weeks of darkness as I brood over the land, having just completed a book, and bombard my editor with second thoughts and third thoughts and corrections and deletions until he or she loses all track of them. I shall not name the beasts over which I have brooded the blackest or various committees may require the return of medals and the few surviving critics who love me may withdraw their affections.

To return to the business of hysteria, which intrigues me. From the standpoint of writing, *Finn's Folly* was an all but overwhelming effort written under pressure of indifferent health at a difficult time, when our youngest child, retarded and hyperactive and then about seven years of age, was dominating the house and not a minute's real relief could be found. Unlike any other book, *Finn's Folly* drained me. I was exhausted and ill when I finished it, but it was about matters very close to home. The Mongol child in the story was of course a fictional recreation of my own daughter. Max's loss of his parents paralleled the death of my father when I was fourteen, yet I saw the death of the parents as my own death, and the children left behind as my own children. The passion that made the book tick, for me, was consuming. And why not? It was my book. I believed I had written a minor masterpiece; it was finished about six months before my doubts became large enough to convince me I was mistaken. Now, I am unable to judge it.

The Fox Hole, by contrast, was written joyously in a few weeks. No effort, just fun, though there was beneath it a hidden, critical decision. I liked *The Fox Hole* when I finished it and I still do.

Chinaman's Reef was laborious and took about nine determined months. After some initial confusion I set out to write a parable about war and *Chinaman's* is how it happened. No apologies. I think it says reasonably well what I meant it to say.

I see no relationship other than the author's name between the three books, yet these are the books in which I am said to be hysterical, a criticism I do not become aggressively outspoken about. After all, if I am accused of hysteria I am not accused of a crime. This is not the sort of thing that sends me running to the woodheap. But it is worth a comment, because I believe it has a bearing upon what I am trying to achieve as a writer and it is only upon my intentions that I can speak with any authority.

If I have acquired any real knowledge in this world it is of the nature and effects of fear. I am not thinking of cowardice. That fear is a profound force in the life of a young person I would have thought self-evident, requiring no explanation beyond the statement, and any mature adult who would attempt to discount it by some alleged process of recollection or psychological insight, is either oddly insensitive or a blowhard. Or, possibly, has led an uncommonly sheltered and unimaginative life.

It seems to me that fear permeates childhood, fear in numerous forms and disguised under numerous names. Have you observed the alarm of a small child lost; not an hour later when he has become used to the idea and accepted a few of the compensations; but the *moment* in which he first knows he is lost? There are many excellent reasons, I think, why this should not be any other way. Fear, like pain, can be a valuable friend as well as a formidable opponent.

My generation knows almost too much about fear and paid a high price for the practical – as opposed to the theoretical – knowledge of it. I flew many operational patrols as a pilot and aircraft captain during the Second World War, flying out from various bases in the British Isles as a member of the Royal Australian Air Force. In each flight I was intensely afraid and I fought this fear all the way out and all the way back, fifty-seven times operationally in flights varying from ten to sixteen hours. Everyone aboard knew that everyone else was afraid – or I assume this was so – but no one demonstrated it visually. Fear, not the enemy, would appear to have been the principal opponent, a devastating opponent. It has left its mark.

As a writer, surfaces fail to involve me. The body is only the shell that carries the person around. Let cameras photograph the body – and I can be moved and excited as a person by what the camera sees of a face or of a body – but not as a writer. In my view the moving picture and the written word travel totally different paths, which may be one of the reasons why I have written something like fifty books and went twenty-seven years as a professional writer before anyone tried to make a film from my work.

When I write of the lights and shades of fear, I write of something belonging to the invisible intensity of being alive. In my own way I am trying to introduce children to the idea that their greatest adventures, their greatest moments, will belong to what goes on inside. Fear is one of these adventures and, paradoxically, is not to be feared; it has the peculiar property of heightening our awareness, of adding brilliance to the mundane, and further depth and dimension to every worthwhile human experience. A surfeit of fear can dull our senses, but no seas were ever lovelier, no skies more magnificent, no hours more crowded with sensual and spiritual wonder than those when as a young man I risked my life day by day. Fear did not turn me off. I lived then in high key, and still do.

You are seeing the inside of my characters, not the outside, so the reader will have to put up with it. I am told this embarrasses some of my English friends. In Britain, apparently, in some quarters, the doctrine of the stiff upper lip worn externally and internally like a steel corset still prevails, no matter how intellectually or emotionally dishonest it may be. I do not see the point.

A novel is a private experience; ideally it is an exchange of the naked truth in the strictest confidence between two sympathetic people. It is not paraded in front of a multitude, it is personal.

I see no reason why a novel principally for boys and girls should be watered down *because* it is a novel for boys and girls. I see no reason why it should be gift-wrapped, or poisoned, or polluted, or should sell out on life, or should call a spade anything other than what it is. If you can turn back the years, if you can honestly peel them off, if you can discard the glow that diffuses the view, you will know that you, too, called a spade a spade when the barriers were down. Even in your innocence you were direct and I take nothing from your innocence by asserting that.

34

There is not much in the world that cannot or does not happen to a child; only in degree does it differ from parallel adult experience, it can indeed be much more frightening. You used to walk tightropes between all kinds of disturbing emotions. If you didn't you could not have been alive. Somehow, childhood must have passed you by. But don't stop the first kid you see in the street and say, "What is it like to be a child?" He is not going to tell you. Even if he could he wouldn't. He is not likely to reveal his secrets to a visitor from another world. If it did not happen to you or if you have forgotten, that's too bad. It's gone. You'll not be finding it again by trying to steer the shortest distance between two points.

The complete adult person should be three creatures at one and the same time; certainly he should be the mature adult, he should also be the young person meeting every fresh experience with delight and surprise, he should also be the child. I like to say to an audience, sometimes, that I stand before you as boy, as youth, as man, and I hope I can go on through life meaning it. True, it's a bit wearing, but what the heck.

So my concern as a writer is not to present children in a form always acceptable to jaded adult taste. I see no reason why it should be. Children on their best behaviour are no doubt ideal pets to have around the house, but these curious and unnatural creatures simply fail to function adequately in the real world where people grow up. Warts and all, I have heard it said of my characters; very well, if that's the curious terminology they prefer, warts and all. I am not interested in preaching sermons to children. I heard thousands between the age of one month and twenty years and remember specifically none. I have preached at least a hundred times myself and thankfully, I suspect, remember little of that either. I am not convinced that a man is then at his best. Nor am I trying to house-train children or to *improve* them. If, quietly, on the side, or round by the back door, or by accident, I help them to grow a little that's a different matter.

I am hoping for characters, perhaps I am *searching* for

characters, that children can identify as human, characters they can understand, with whom they can sympathize, or with whom they can themselves identify. Out of this type of shared experience a boy or a girl might catch on to the idea that trying to know your friend is better than judging him. They might come around to the idea that all kinds of people have all kinds of problems, grown-up people even, and other kids, and his or her personal load of guilt or doubt or anxiety might begin to weigh a little less. Yet this is not the primary aim; perhaps it is pompous to have an aim at all; if it is possible to express a *hope* in words, it is simply to continue a shared journey of discovery into the wonderland of human experience.

I do not expect any child to read all my books, those that might be said to begin with *Hills End*; I would be honoured, but I would not expect or hope for it. Kids should get out into the open fields and come home laden with an armful of assorted blooms, with all the wonderful things of good fantasy and recreated history and poetic imagery and high adventure and nature. If, in the course of a childhood, three or four Southalls come home in the bunch I am happy. As for the adults who read me, sympathetically or otherwise, I hope that one of these days someone will try to see my work as a whole and not as a collection of parts. I hope that some will see how this journey of discovery is moving in many directions and certain directions are destined from the outset to be less rewarding than others, but the journey must be made, nevertheless.

Within the limits of my capacity I endeavour to make each journey with a boy and a girl beside me. I see them there. I feel them there. If occasionally my stride is too long and they have to stretch, it will not be the last time they are required to run to keep up with a man who is intent upon taking them somewhere.

3 Call It a Wheel: Where Books Come From

The following memoir was written for *The Horn Book Magazine*, fiftieth anniversary issue, October 1974. This version carries some revisions.

I have spent some time lately wrestling with the problem of beginnings. I solved the problem of endings long ago by agreeing with myself that there was no such animal as an ending to anything. So it was logical that sooner or later I would come to beginnings. Naturally, I have arrived at the same kind of understanding; beginnings are as elusive as endings and will not submit to capture or definition, life and literature apparently being parts of a continuing state of now. This is another way of suggesting that cause and effect are infinite and eternal – and *that* is another way of saying that the whole thing is beyond me.

I do not present this pronouncement as a philosophical breakthrough of importance, but as evidence of the agony some writers are required to go through to reach conclusions that are self-evident to others. I am not complaining: for me this agony is the joy, the discipline, the substance, and the growth of every book for children I am content to put my name on. In other words, I do not mind being slow-witted; far from being a handicap, slow-wittedness enables me to go on through life discovering wonderful things almost constantly, wholly untroubled by the probability that everyone else already knows them. If I were an inventor, I am sure I would be at the brink of cutting the end off a log and calling it a wheel.

In the light shed by these meditations I have been wondering where *Josh* came from. I mean, people ask you; they expect you to know; they *expect* beginnings. So this is bound to be an exercise in frustration if I am to take any notice of myself, yet an alluring invitation just the same.

The origins of *Josh* are harder to put a finger on than say, *Hills End* or *Ash Road* or *The Fox Hole* or *Over the Top*. These four books sprang in significant part from recognizable events of my adult life, and it is possible to isolate particular incidents and say, "Yes, something started moving there", although each incident ended up like a cottage pie with bits of everything in it, including the sweepings off the pantry shelf and all the herbs in the garden. It would have been so much easier to have written about any one, or all, of them than about *Josh*. Why must one inevitably pick the hard way?

Over the Top emerged from the birth of one of my children and from the rugged, primitive, and sometimes bitter life I was subjecting my family to at the time, miles from anywhere – in the wild, close to nature, close to the earth. (But the older children remember the life with great affection.) *The Fox Hole* grew from our adventures with a mysterious hole in the ground that evoked disquieting issues of decision and direction; a fortune – *or what?* – lay only inches from me. *Ash Road* was generated by fire, by the emotional shock of the most devastating forest fire I ever wish to know about and from which we escaped as a family in the middle of a frightening night, groping uphill behind headlight beams into a stifling smoke fog, with the world around us thundering and flaming with overwhelming sound. *Hills End* began to appear out of the routine of each day, out of the realization, unexpectedly come upon, that I had wasted half a lifetime searching for treasure already held in my hands.

None of these books happened in a few minutes, nor were they born fully formed. The gestation period, before I wrote a word of any one of them, ranged from a year to twenty years, but all were strongly related in physical terms. The originating incidents all happened in real life on that hungry little farm down a lonely road, where we struggled through an engrossing experience of fourteen years, sometimes savouring its magic, but never fully comprehending its complexity until after we drove away. As far as I know, *Josh* had but little to do with that.

Perhaps *Josh* began to move one January day in 1943. An act of foolishness I have not chosen to look directly at before this moment. What was it? A masquerade, a posturing, an absurdity or an escape? Hence young men die. A pilot in training, that was I. A natural swimming pool in the hills outside Adelaide, dark waters, overcast sky, with fellow-trainees, four or five, and people I didn't know, and girls on the grassy banks around admiring us obliquely, admiring the others, anyway. I was too thin to be happily observed. Held myself well in uniform, looked straight and square and tall, but in swimming trunks it was another tale. Why was I there? Heaven knows. Compromised, I suppose, and too embarrassed or ashamed to admit I had never learnt to swim because I felt my body was too thin to display. In dived the others at the deep end, those four or five air force trainees, watched by the girls, and in dived I. For God's sake why?

How long was I there? I cannot say. Water enveloping me, coldness and blackness and no way through. I could not see and never knew whether I was on the surface or ten feet down. I made all the swimming motions I had ever known, but nothing logical occurred, and every part of me gasped for air. Lungs and muscles and rhythms implored me to breathe, and I had to gulp the water to fill the hole inside. So I breathed at water, in and out, deep down, and what was my mother going to say, and wasn't the whole thing mad; dying in a puddle from nothing but pride? Alan Perry came and punched me in the jaw and dragged me to ground, and where the water went from inside I don't really know.

After a while, Alan Perry said (he was older than I), "That was stupid." He said it and frowned. So I sat on the grass for the rest of the afternoon, a wet towel over my shoulders.

Or had *Josh* begun to move earlier than that?

I was eight, I think.

Sitting up in bed playing with words:

Spring is a happy season
Cold old winter has gone
The birds begin to build their nests
Up in the trees so high
Spring is happiest and the best
Of all the seasons that go by.

"Dad," I said, when he came in to tip me out for school, "I've made up a poem."

I recited it to him, and he said, "You didn't really make it up, did you? That's someone else's poem. That's dishonest. That's the same as stealing, son."

"I made it up," I said.

He was a good man, but I know he did not believe me then.

It might have been later when *Josh* stirred. Much later, 1950 or 1951.

Our farm, down that lonely road, and a friend had come.

"Look," the friend said, "those old rabbit traps in the shed. Why don't you set them? Why go without meat? Bunny's good."

"It's never occurred to me," I said.

"Don't you know how?"

I shook my head.

"Come on, then. We'll set them now. There's nothing to it. Southall, you're dumb."

He set them on a track through the scrub, a narrow track, narrower by far than men need for themselves, set them there and lightly covered them with dust and leaves and twigs.

"Isn't it indiscriminate?" I said. "Who says it'll not be a dog or a wallaby or a cat?"

"Rabbits are stupid," he said.

At dusk I heard the scream. "My God," I said, "what's that?"

We ran all the way from the house, down the hill, into the bush, with a smoking hurricane lamp hurriedly lit to throw a ray of light and an old axe handle for a club. And that rabbit went on screaming until he saw the light and heard us come.

Or do we go a long way back instead, back to the stirrings of awareness, to that curious shift between not knowing what happened yesterday and an understanding that being alive is more than a mindless flowering?

Can we ever begin to express the wonder of this awakening or the warmth of the recall when we break back through again? "Yes, I could not have been much past three years of age; yet I do remember being there, I do remember saying it, I do remember feeling isn't this good. *I was there*, and I knew it at the time, and remember it still." Great Aunt Susan happens way back then where the mist clears and the sun comes up bright red.

She swept out of Heaven knew where, dressed in black, with a sense of style and a sense of drama and enormously old (all of sixty, I guess), the Queen of Hearts, the Queen of Diamonds, undisputed mistress wherever she trod. That was how I saw her, however much to adult eyes she might have fallen short of that. It never mattered what others thought of her; it never mattered how others saw her; no one else in the world knew her as I knew her; Auntie Susie was mine. I am incapable of judging her even yet.

There she knelt on my mother's bedroom floor – I could show you the spot still, even though walls have moved in the house – knelt there opening a large travelling bag and taking from it the first magic tracing book I ever owned; there might have been others, but they never registered, never left an impression, because they had not come from her. I loved her then, from that day. Instant rapport. You know, I'm sure. With a few people in a lifetime, allowing for no barriers, age or distance or class or kind. What happened with Auntie Susie had nothing to do with tracing books, or pennies, or bribery and corruption of any sort.

Again and again as I grew, I went to see her, once with my parents, every other time travelling the hundred and one miles alone; eight miles by suburban electric train, seventy-two miles by steam train, twenty-one miles by motor train. But not as often as I hoped; the fare was little enough in those days – seventeen shillings return – but we were poor.

Oh, the adventure of those journeys to the uttermost ends of the earth; the great trestle bridges, the horseshoe bends – the tail of the train across the valley miraculously travelling the opposite way, the deeply-rooted thud of the rails that was inside you like a heartbeat, the sharp soots in your eye, the half-eaten apple going brown because you could not bring yourself to miss another moment of the fabulous world outside, throwing out the newspapers and the cheap weekly magazines, paper blooming into the air across paddocks and scrubland for the country people to pick up and take home. There they stood waving as the great train went by, as if you or they were not quite real. There ran the bush kids falling behind, shrill voices calling across space and time for comics to read. It was good to catch a smile.

The one-car motor train, boarded in the cave beneath the far-up girders at Ballarat, the great city in the west with gold in the streets. (Ballarat, seen through the aura of years.) Walked with my head down along blue-stone gutters and bitumen footpaths looking for the glint. That incredible train that carried you over the last twenty-one miles, twenty-one miles more on into the west. Grown-ups hated the thing (even Auntie Susie did not appreciate it much), but for a kid there was wonder inside that bus, in its grotesqueness, its hard discomfort, its rattling and its pitching and its swaying and its dust, with the driver up front where you could see him, even talk to him if you were very brave. Auntie Susie meeting it at the end of the line, the uttermost end of the earth. Almost too much for the young mind. Almost too much for one day. Excitement all the way. Excitement to be there. Excitement because it was her.

Walking up the hill together, hand in arm, into the warm evening, as if you had changed dimensions, as if perhaps Heaven were only a train-ride from home. The smell of cows and wattle blossom and the wood smoke of fires. The tension building because in a moment you would be *there*.

That unforgettable house of hers. Was it real? Did I invent it or imagine it or convert it? Was it there as I saw it, or was it never there at all? Dark timbers and creaking boards, dried-flower arrangements in picture-frames – enormous things of enormous complexity. Where can they be now? How can it all be no more? Even the pedal organ clacking and wheezing and making aeroplane noises for me by the hour. I must have driven her mad.

Cornish pasties and egg and bacon pie, lavender bags everywhere, clocks chiming, candle flames. Fishing for perch, idling, with the wind singing in the pines, six feet of bamboo plucked from her garden and a hook and a piece of twine. The smell of old shops, little shops, just two or three; was it cinnamon I could smell or old wool or old varnish or dead men's dreams? Merchandise made years before and never sold, wonderful old labels (an art lost, an art squandered, an art insensitively thrown away), cures for all ills; somehow grown dark and forgotten and unused, shutters up outside to the heat and the street with dead men's names flaking away.

Jogging for miles in the sun with the baker at my side, sometimes holding the reins behind the horse's switching tail. "Gidee-ap there, old Jo. Go." Bread for gold miners and spinster ladies of outspoken religious convictions and impoverished settlers stricken by depression struggling to live off yellow clay.

A lean-limbed girl with a straight back and a proud walk and dark hair and brown eyes and exciting poise. I longed for her to be my friend, longed to hold her hand, to feel its warmth and clasp and life in mine; to rest my face at her cheek was the most improbable dream, so intoxicating my senses reeled; but never was I able to utter an intelligent word. I would think of her all year long, or over two years or three, until I went back again. But never spoke a word to her except *hullo*. Then watched her go.

A dam, a yellow dam for swimming in if you were not me, three strong boys there, unclothed, running unashamed, the first nakedness clearly exposed I ever saw except my own.

Bible reading by lantern light and learning long psalms by heart to please her. Wanting only to please her all the time. Singing hymns beside her at the organ even after my voice broke and became a croaking sound. Going away from her, sadly going home, perhaps for ever. Who could be sure? Farther and farther away from her on the hillside, harder and harder to see her there, flapping her tablecloth up and down, up and down. I was off to war, as I thought to die, but death came to her.

Flapping the tablecloth up and down, the last of her I saw. Good-bye.

That was when *Josh* started, I suppose, and other things beside.

4 Something Like a Love Affair

This lecture began as a talk prepared for the South
Australian Writers' Fellowship and delivered in
Adelaide on 19 May 1973. Considerably developed,
it was next presented on 12 November 1973, at the
Library of Congress, Washington, D.C., under the
auspices of the Gertrude Clarke Whittall Poetry
and Literature Fund, in observance of National
Children's Book Week. It was recorded for radio
and television and published in the *Quarterly
Journal of the Library of Congress*, April 1974.
Further revisions and additions have been made.

I am setting out to try to say something about books for children
as I see them, and as I would like more to be, but it has to be
seen as a personal statement, not as an attempt to persuade or
convert others. This is simply my own view of my own road,
and for me it's fine, but because I am a writer I address much
of what I say to writers and to people who are interested in
what writers do and how writers of my kind might work. I have
tried to look at the creative process as I know it, without
burning into it to depths that might destroy it, or inhibit its
future functions. I also chuck a few bricks through a few
windows because I think it's time.

To begin, I chuck a brick through a window of my own
house. There is a continuing tendency in my country to regard
the writing of books for children, and the various professions
and vocations arising from the original creative act, as occu-
pations suitable for minor-type, mouse-sized humans whose
passions bubble at less than normal adult heat. Nowhere is this
view more often aired than in the "world of literature". Writers,
publishers, critics, lecturers, and pressmen of various kinds not

actively occupied in the creation or appreciation of children's literature *as* it is, go on failing to comprehend *what* it is. Echoes of this same attitude probably go on reverberating everywhere else.

The viewpoint mystifies me – that modern works for children must necessarily be minor works by minor writers, that deliberately they are generated and projected at reduced voltage, that they evade truth, that they avert passion and sensuality and the subtleties of life and are unworthy of the attention of the serious creative writer – artist or craftsman.

The sensitive child, the core of everything that I, for one, wish to write about, is the direct antithesis of this milk and water proposition. Adult scaling-down of the intensity of the child state is an outrageous distortion of what childhood is all about, and simply having to put the idea into words is ludicrous. Why should it need expression? Since when has physical frailty been weakness; since when has timidity been bracketed with spinelessness; since when have delicate sensitivities come to be regarded as sentimental trivialities? These qualities are part of childhood along with those other aspects that are as rumbustious as run-away bulls. I am nonplussed.

As we grow older it seems to me we look back more and more, *not*, I suspect, because a mature person really wishes again for the agonies and ecstasies of youth in the immediate sense, but because of the need to recall the enormous impact, the enormous importance, the sheer magnitude of childhood events to compensate for the lower key of subsequent adult life. I am sure it is not unreasonable to suggest that they are recalled because they are worthy of recall, because little else in life surpasses them.

I would go a stage further and suggest that it is possible to extend the intensity of a sensitive childhood into maturity, without wearing yourself out or giving yourself ulcers or coronaries or other undesirable side-effects, although it may add to the daily anguishing of your heart. I am not sure that anguish is all that bad. Was there ever any joy worth having that did not exact a price?

46

I suppose it would be "scientifically untenable" to recommend children's literature, so-called, as a suitable physic for ageing spirits? I make the recommendation, nevertheless. The creation of it and the appreciation of it at a significant level is one way of charging adult life with some of the extra sensual dimensions of childhood. Someone long ago, in different words, made a related statement and it is the key, from where I look at life, to being alive from the tips of your toes to the hair of your head and to every nerve-end in between.

Not all share this partisan opinion.

I recall a literary function in Sydney during one of my visits there. Members of a writers' society were the hosts, I was the guest (or the *excuse*), and *To The Wild Sky*, written in 1965, had just been named Australian Children's Book of the Year, 1968. A lady novelist ran me into a corner. This lady may have lifted me by the lapel, I do not swear to it, but I swear to the essence of what she said: "I can't understand, I can't you know, how a grown-up adult with literary equipment can waste his talent writing nice little stories for children, when the world is full of man-size problems demanding all the enlightenment the novelist can shed upon them."

It's an interesting viewpoint and I have gone on thinking about it, gone on considering it, and gone on mentioning it at every opportunity, but only critics have ever come near to convincing me she might have been right – yet not for the reasons used by them to discipline me.

I "fixed" the lady in the eye and asked her, "Have you read anything lately that children are reading?" A fair enough question, I thought, but she passed it over without a spoken comment. "My God," her expression implied. "What do you take me for?"

Out on the fringes of the field of the writing game, way out where the vague boundary line between player and spectator begins to diffuse, are those people, those numerous people, who write for children the stories they are sure children will enjoy, because they have told them to children gathered round them to the sound of crackling wood fires or to the beating of moth-wings against wire-screens on long summer evenings. Mistakenly, they attribute the glow of those occasions to the magic of the story and forget the crucial contribution of the warmth of voice and smile and body and glance and that bedtime was being effectively deferred. Their success was a human success growing out of the aura of love – and that should have been enough. But they turn a wonderful memory into a pain. Upon the cold page in cold print the magic is not there. Human love is no longer present to overwhelm the defects. Sadly, for themselves, they are misled as to the quality of their talent and wastefully go ahead to misuse their own precious time, and wastefully to expend the time of publishers and others, and wastefully to inflict the subsequent bewilderments and agonies of their wounded egos upon people like me who generally are too polite to protest.

Manuscripts come to me for my *honest* opinion – something I would never dare give whilst valuing friendship or the quiet life. I learnt quickly that the word *honest* is used strictly in an illusionary sense. Hell hath no fury like the writer seeking honesty, and who gets it.

These manuscripts come through the post or through friends or are delivered by hand – after every publisher in the country has rejected them – all too often accompanied by letters running something like this:

The enclosed story is adored by my grandchildren. Everyone says it should be published. No one can understand why it has not been published. Every publisher who has sent it back has enthused about it. I enclose photostat copies of seventeen of their letters for you to read. Don't you agree it is a shame for this beautiful story to be wasted? It is because I am not known and am without influence and do not have friends in the right places. Why don't you put it into a book with your name on it? No one will pick the difference and hundreds of thousands of children all over the world will be as happy as my grandchildren.

Sometimes these letters send my blood pressure up. It

depends upon the day. But why do people go on being so ignorant of the craft they pretend to practise when an hour of honest self-scrutiny in the reflection of what children's literature really is would surely convince them not only of their weakness but of their unreasonable vanity? But they do not judge themselves by the best; they shut their souls to that; they read the worst and say, "I can do better than that." And so the worst goes on propagating itself like a geometric progression of splitting cells, yet upon reflection these people sadden me and I cannot bring myself to hurt them. Life is more than blunt reaction. Life goes farther than what we know to be simple, obvious common sense. There they lie, naked, already hurt enough, so I add my own little white lie to the rest and sometimes bring upon myself most complex human complications that have taken months of my life to put straight, but I doubt if at heart I have regretted it once.

Here I would like to frame a definition, an explanation, a statement; call it what you wish. It is my response to adult novelists who do not understand and to others who should understand: I do not regard writing for children as a minor sub-division of literature, I do not regard it as a special sub-division of literature, I reject the *term sub-division*. When, as a writer, I address myself to children's literature, as now, I address myself to literature; and when as a writer I address myself to children I address myself to equals. I see no conflict of definition, and if I have a philosophy, as a writer for children, that is it. It is my philosophy, my viewpoint, and it is not likely to change if no one else supports it. The clauses in smaller print we will come to later.

Perhaps I should make it clear that this has little to do with the nature of my relationships with children face to face – as in a classroom or assembly hall situation where I often meet children – or in family or personal situations. As most of us are, I am split in parts; one part obviously a parent, sometimes strait-laced, sometimes "compassionate" to the point of indulgence; in another part I am obviously an uninhibited

49

entertainer; and in another I am wholly *with* the child, in the pages of a book my heart beats with the pulse of a child, I believe I then become a child.

It is upon that fact, the valid artistic achievement of identification, that I see children's literature as literature in its own right, yet I admit the need in the organized world of books for classification. Children, for instance, should know where the books most likely to please them are kept, or else libraries become disorderly houses, though many books that belong where the children browse belong also where the grown-ups browse, even if it is not common for them to be found in those areas. I am assured by critics who read widely in both fields, that the best children's books often have more to say than their adult counterparts. Fortunately for children, children's librarians are generally rather a special breed, not at all reluctant to shop widely, not shy to pick the flowers from the fields where adult books grow; but the other way around it is a less catholic tale.

There was a time, and not long ago, when I regarded writing for kids as a fit and proper occupation only for a bandaged left hand, as a kind of lightly entertaining break every second year or so from the serious business of writing for adults. It is scarcely surprising that others not sharing my background or commitment should think of books for children generally as being beneath the serious attention of the writer and unworthy of serious consideration as literature in an adult world – the great works of the past excepted. Antiquity somehow lends stature to literature whether it rightly deserves it or not. Accidents of survival happen.

A letter from a friend this very day, received almost at this word, deplores the standard of children's books going into braille in her particular part of the world. Very low literary standard, she says, entirely visual books, action books, twee books, nothing that breathes of the soul and the spirit, nothing that stirs to the sensuality of smell and sound and touch, and are they not the qualities to give the child who has no sight?

It is not that the right books do not exist; it is simply that the people who choose the books are ignorant or conservative to the point of archaic caution. Choice, in their terms, I would call chance.

A well-known journalist, respected for her perceptive interviews, expressed with irony her surprise during our one short conversation that I appeared to be implying that significant writers were seriously involved in the creation of books for children. I got the feeling that in her view she was operating at less than her proper capacity by giving time to me. Her irony still was evident in the patronizing piece published later; there she used it to cut me down to size. Yet people of her kind, involved with literature, do not snatch barbs like these out of the air. Her mind was closed, it is true, but why? Certainly not because the children's books she knew had impressed her with their grandeur or beauty or elegance. I would suggest she had not read any in a long time or had come to books for children in an unkindly selective, unsympathetic or hostile frame of mind. It would need more than her word to convince me she had read me: perhaps she had scanned the publisher's blurb of two or three.

Sometimes I say to people, "I know there are not enough hours in the day or enough days in a life to read everything you should not miss, but can't you come once in a while with an open heart and an open mind to a good children's book about childhood that reputation tells you has made the grade? You might be surprised by the substance you take away."

How much has society's laboured misreading of a well-known text from St Paul cut off adult man and woman from many of the sensual wonderments of life, or, at best, has muted the appreciation or diluted the appreciation of emotions and sensations and events that should have *excited* them to the bloodstream. The young person is forever being urged to grow up and there is a carry-over of this unthinking indoctrination into adult life that desensitizes people. *Immature* is the word I read on a school report in 1968 referring to one of my daughters then nine years of age. What does God have in mind for a girl to be at nine years of age?

Putting away childish things, surely, has nothing to do with putting away the child. It is a total distortion of terms. The child should go on inside you helping you to reach out to each new emotion, helping you to excite to each new encounter, helping you to delight unconditionally to each new experience of the senses. Godfathers; why should it be considered an unendurable or unacceptable strain? Given reasonable health, are seventy years or eighty years too many to handle when it has taken four billion years to prepare the place where you stand?

People have said to me, "It's all right for you to take that attitude. That's easy when you're on top. That's easy when you've got a carpet on the floor. That's easy when you've never had to soil your hands."

Life can be a rugged experience. I am aware of it. It is the kind of life I have lived, but the child in me is relatively intact. It is an inner quality, not worn externally, not always visible externally, a very personal matter. Perhaps it is why I write for children, though I prefer to say it has happened to me *because* I write for children, and this I would wish for other writers of serious intent to enjoy. It comes so close to the core of all creativity, and this brings me to the threshold of thoughts I am anxious to express well: how is it that an adult of mature years and tastes and appetites can sustain the state of mind and emotion and simplicity that writing about children for children obviously requires? Is it an agony? Is it worth it? Is it a bore? Is there a measure by which one may say it is proper activity for a serious writer? Or does one come to it simply because there is nowhere else to go; does one home in upon one's *métier* instinctively? Each to his own?

Creative writing for children does require a particular facility, but the writer is not likely to dig it out of himself roots and stalk and blossom fully grown. Neither is he likely to write for the theatre, nor for the sports page, without the revelant aptitude. Good writing for children is a discipline of specific subtleties arising out of awarenesses most laboriously sought, but joyously found, and the best of it stands unblushingly as literature beside the best of anything. The worst of it should be sunk with a millstone in the sea.

I become irritable and intolerant when confronted by the smooth-tongued purveyors of the blatantly commercial second-rate. "We are giving them what they want," is the alleged doctrine of these people. I do not believe *they* want it for a moment and would never miss it if it were not there. But it *is* there and what do we do about it? No good ignoring it, because it stays there, waxing stronger. I suppose, with some subtlety, we have to join it; ladders to better things have to be dropped in amongst it. There might be some difficult decisions.

The blatant second-raters dish up what is easiest to concoct, or what careless or unthinking or ignorant adults are prepared to accept without question or exercise of discernment for their children or grandchildren or nieces or nephews, or, Heaven forbid, for their students.

The pulp trade for kids is gigantic. It prospers on apathy and sells by the truck-load because it sets up in the market-place where the public gathers with the pay-day dollar. And people get what they bargain for – the superficially pretty book, the lazy book, the formula book, the patronizing book, and some-one must be making a wad of money out of it, though I doubt if much of this finds its way to the initial creators. In my view, these people, both creators and publishers, have to be called the ultimate cynics.

The producer of the honest second-rate is another matter. Time and persistence and conscience may yet make something of him, though not necessarily. One must never forget one's own origins, nor deny them, whether they were honest or not. They are part of you. Perhaps they made you. Or perhaps they held you back.

I would like to define, from my narrow viewpoint, what a good children's book is not. I am not inferring that bad or dis-honest children's books will cripple the finer instincts for ever and will not give some poor little innocents their modicum of moderate pleasure, but good children's books available at the same price, or less, in paperback, would have given the same children so much more. And I do not mean more in the sense that these children know it from the corruptive, insidious and sickening materialism of much mass-media advertising and virtually all mass-media give-aways, those daily doses of perversion administered in the privacy of their own homes, under the non-seeing eyes and non-hearing ears of their parents.

A good children's book is not an imitation of something else, not an imitation of last year's Newbery or last year's Carnegie, not an imitation of Walt Disney, not an imitation of Lewis Carroll, not intellectually or emotionally or artistically shoddy. It does not, inevitably, sugar the pill of life. It does not manipulate or indoctrinate. It is not Public Relations copy for anybody or anything, or sooner or later it is the sick victim of its own infection. It does not necessarily begin with *once upon a time*, nor necessarily end with *happily ever after*.

It is, as you can see, demonstrably easy to string a list of negatives together, but much more difficult to define what a good children's book actually is. Over it will almost certainly hang controversy and passions that comparable literature intended for adults rarely provokes. Thank God, it is almost impossible to define the positives, or some smart alec would long ago have programmed a computer. It remains an intensely human matter of creation and choice and approval, and original works for children, like exotic flowers, are springing up all over the world. Never before, as far as I know, have writers succeeded so often with brilliance.

Is it possible then to define the writer who can reach children? I mean *reach*, as opposed to entertain mildly or superficially amuse. May we, in doing so, come closer to a definition of a good book by looking along another sight?

Any writer who considers himself too sensitive or too subtle or too significant or too mature or simply too brilliant to write for children, is undoubtedly a person of keen self-perception.

54

And for any writer who has discovered that the big bad man-size world is a bit beyond him and feels that the time has come to set his objectives a little lower, I would suggest that he should do so.

If I am able to define the writer for children, I believe he is a person who can identify with children, consciously or sub-consciously, and can project his images through the written word in such a way that children can identify with him. Here we run into a problem of word usage. *Identify*. The terms identify and identification have become tired clichés – as so many beautiful terms have become through misuse. The inference of the meaning of these words has degenerated to a kind of second-rate emotional twitch, part of the phony culture. I am talking of a genuine emotion, a genuine and huge transformation of one's personal attitudes as an adult back into a genuine re-experience of one's personal attitudes as a child.

The children's writer does not write for all children any more than the writer for adults writes for all adults. Over and over again I have to say that. You reach those and please those who tune in on your wavelength. It is a very personal matter. Rapport – no less and probably no more. If it is not there the reader is wasting his time. If it is there, it is something like a love affair, and even children fall in love.

It is an absurdity of much criticism that one adult person can declare the judgement that a book will not appeal to children – in the plural, in the mass. There are factors involved here, there are vanities and assumptions that perturb me, because the influence of some of these people is out of all proportion to their stature. They can almost kill a book. They can crush a writer's spirit.

In 1968, during the course of accepting an award, I said publicly that beyond the writer, between him and the child, there had grown a barbed wire entanglement through which the book, beating with the writer's blood, had to thrust its way. Sometimes a book might breast the entanglement and drive on joyfully to meet the child; sometimes the book fell half-way, all bloodied and torn. Colourful metaphors, perhaps, but true enough just the same. Usually if a book falls it has earned its fair reward, but mistakes can be made. Sometimes the book that breasts the entanglement is not the one that deserves to live and afterwards promptly dies, to prove it, and the other fights on and breaks through and lives for a generation. Picking the survivors in advance is all but impossible.

I felt brave enough at the time to urge the critics present not to be widely generous with their praise, unless by chance they encouraged a writer who had entirely mistaken his direction and would be better working elsewhere. And I urged them that in the critical exercise of their wit not to go too far the other way and perhaps break the spirit of another writer who might be stumbling in a wilderness only a year or two short of power. Perhaps it was caddish to point out that the writing of a book, however ill-conceived, was rarely less than the labour of months, whereas the writing of a critique, however scintillating, was rarely more than the labour of a few days.

There are writers who assure me that the views expressed by critics mean nothing to them. In the long view I suspect this to be a defence for wounded souls. My own painful evolution as a writer for children has laid me open to a great deal of criticism (which continues) and I believe at different times I have recited the old one about sticks and stones that break the body but criticism bounces off. This has always been an over-simplification.

A writer cannot thrive in a destructively hostile environment, nor, I suppose, can the critic. A writer bares his soul at some personal risk to produce a significant work; the critic in his own way must go equally as far if he is to enjoy the satisfaction of fulfilling a constructive function.

It is fashionable in Australia, and probably elsewhere, to deny that one writes for children specifically, one writes for people, but I cannot hang my hat on that hook. One does write for children, in a certain difficult-to-define way. Then there is a strong school of criticism directed against some writers because they write about children rather than for them. The subtlety of this distinction has always eluded me. I have to say that the writer for children, as I know him, is very much committed to writing about children. Am I mistaken, or is childhood not lived by children?

Present-day literate children, under the guidance of sensitive teachers and librarians, helped by the reactions of responsible critics, expect more than the old sentimental sweetness, the old super heroes, the old exploits of middle or upper class children solving crimes and accomplishing deeds beyond the intelligence or courage or capacity of grown-ups. We are now writing for what is the largest literate open-hearted audience in the history of the world. I would not try to calculate how many of these children I have met in recent years face to face or through correspondence. I begin most working-days by answering their letters. We are not committed to a non-caring, disinterested, apathetic, brassed-off audience. At the risk of sounding trite or cosy, we are committed to the hope of the world – and should never for a moment forget it.

As for the *ill*-literate children I regret as much as anyone that it appears there is not much the serious writer can do. I have anguished over it, I have been asked to write in simplified English, to confine myself to set vocabularies, to limit themes and avoid abstracts, but I have always in the end refused, not able to convince myself that the specialist editors and educationalists concerned were beyond challenge in their views. I stick to my instinct that the person who is not going to read is not going to read, and that the person who *is* going to read, eventually, will get there on his own terms. The experts can probably produce masses of statistical bullets to shoot me down; they're welcome, that's their privilege; but I keep to my instinct that we are trying to turn uncomplicated people into what they are not, and we go on adding to their lives' tensions and anxieties and pressures and difficulties they do not need and would be much happier without.

The serious creative writer cannot and must not reduce his

standards to a lower common denominator. I know some are trying to do this, from high motives, but I believe they are in error. You cannot go back; you are writing down. A writer's earlier works reissued, and possibly re-edited to present-day standards, may serve as a bridge. At least it is an honest bridge, and I have allowed it to happen. Rightly or wrongly, time will tell. But, as I see it, immediately the creative writer consciously reduces his standards for new work, consciously stoops, he loses his stature. His disciplines collapse. His literary judgements desert him. The good writer, despite himself, can produce a load of rubbish.

It is the responsibility, however difficult, of the teacher to bring the marginal child up to the writer, to whatever level the particular writer functions at. The writer cannot legitimately go down. Yet there are other children who never can and never will come up to meet the writer. To take an extreme case, my own youngest child at home, now aged twelve, cannot write or read or speak and probably never shall. There is nothing I can write for her that I will know beyond doubt she understands. We are not born intellectually or emotionally equal. But this child of ours will drag us by the hand across the garden to a flower, and for hours will watch the moon, her eyes radiant.

The only way the writer can reach the marginal children is by going out physically to meet them, to meet *all* children, and people such as I often do, but to acquit oneself adequately takes years of practice, of disciplining nerves and self-consciousness, even of subduing one's proper modesty, but I do see it as an exciting and rejuvenating part of the life of the writer, even though in the immediate sense it can be an exhausting ordeal.

I go out, certainly twice in every year, into culturally deprived or geographically remote areas for the Australian Literature Board, supplied with a car of government origin and a driver escort (usually an adult education officer or a librarian), to meet up with schoolchildren by the score or by the hundred several times in every school day over two or even three successive weeks, often speaking to their parents at night, and travelling in between in stages probably several hundred miles in each day.

One goes out to these kids to stir them up, to entertain them, to bring them something they haven't seen before, and this sort of stimulation given only once can set the gifted child on his way, or bring the backward or reluctant reader finally to the printed page, but there that lass or lad has to discover, perhaps with disappointment that the writer on paper is not the same as the writer who clowned in the classroom or on the school stage. To the novelist, as such, I fear, large numbers of children are lost and if he tries to reach them in print he does so at peril. If he reaches them by striking a responsive chord, hallelujah, but that is another matter. It is true that each of us lives in a different world, and there are as many worlds as persons, and as many needs. Every consciousness and every encounter is unique; a fairly obvious kind of statement; but from time to time it can throw up a few surprises. No one knows what is waiting to be found, even in his own mind, until he explores.

I cannot see how the writer for children, for his own sake, can consider the risk of consciously compromising an intellectual principle, or of committing the patronage of consciously contriving character or incident to tie up a knot or to meet a specification, or of consciously considering the boy or girl who is to read him as other than his equal. You are aware of him as a child, but never as an iddy biddy little kiddie. He can always go back a page and pick you up again if he's in doubt. If he can't be bothered to go back a page then clearly, in his case, it doesn't matter anyway.

As I see it, the writer is on his honour to extend his creative capacities always to the limit. If he does not, he is betraying himself. Talents grow from stretching, not from squeezing into corners. The writer may use language as he wishes, grandly or daringly or poetically or experimentally. He may be as different as his theme moves him to be. He is deluded if he believes he is creatively inhibited or caged or finds himself wondering whether his genius is going to waste on pint-sized mentalities. The kids in tune with him will be up there with him. Critics may tell him he is writing over their heads. Children will send letters with love to say, "Thank you for opening my eyes." If some children *are* left confused or wondering or frustrated by what he has given them, he should not allow himself to become upset about it. Life is like that: some people can cope with given situations, others can't. No man can (or should be asked) to carry the cares of the world, nor should he be condemned because there are people who react unfavourably to him. Yet one must *qualify* that.

Think on the complexities of your readership. Every day someone coming to you for the first time. Always someone growing, evolving, as you draw him into your idea of the world. A readership not set in its ways, its tastes not formed, its opinions not determined. One must tread with care. This can become (if one allows it) an all but daunting challenge to creativity and decision, yet I do not see that the closed roads and detours impose restrictions that are unacceptable to a free, creating spirit. They provoke him. They stimulate him. Certainly the mainstream of present-day writing for adults might indicate that novelists are superbly liberated, or possibly it indicates something else, a sort of uncaring, unthinking, undisciplined pitching of paint at a wall that later generations may scrape off.

What I wish for the writer for children – what I wish for myself – is the ultimate compliment, the return of the reader in his maturity to the same book, with new insight, new discovery, new joy. I would not wish for the writer for children – or for me – that the reader in maturity should come back with the accusation: "You deceived me. You sold me short. You did not write from your heart. You wrote in a hurry off the top of your head."

What does one write for children?

One does best to meet the question obliquely. Immediately a definition is framed one proposes a limitation. It is better to liberate the writer, to open a door and show him the world.

I hesitate to accept that there can be a significant difference, at heart, where it counts, between modern children and the rest of the kids who have gone swarming across this planet since men and women long ago started waking up to the miracle of being. We all have in common our childhood, this extra-ordinary, overwhelming occurrence, this progress of the pilgrim seed through years of gathering awareness. And most of us have in common a tragic capacity to forget what childhood is about. We leap into the luxury of grown-up liberty and allow the impact of life and events upon children to sink at once into a shadowed area. We ignore the truth (sometimes until violently reminded) that anything that can happen to a grown person can happen to a person not grown. We forget the vividness and brilliance and breathtaking wonderment of the world a kid finds each morning when he slams the door and rushes out. We forget its terror, its violence, its bewilderment, except in the sense that we feel children should be shielded and sheltered from all these things, that voices should not be raised in anger or serious dispute in their hearing, and that the substance of reality should somehow be disguised when children are present. There is a certain irrationality about this. We rear them upon impossible simplicities that must confuse them profoundly, that life consists of opposites; dark, light; dull, bright; bad, good; wrong, right; and that parents are all-wise and all-knowing and sinless.

We expend great labours during a child's early years in-fluencing him, one way or the other, and he spends his youth reversing the procedure. If we raise a healthy pagan, he goes searching for God; if we raise a healthy Methodist, my sainted aunt, one hardly dares picture him on the loose. When you write for children about life, how can you depict it as anything other than you know it to be? To fail is simply to be guilty of deceit. To fail is to mislead. The ultimate judgement on issues and events must be left to the children who read you, no matter how long it takes them in terms of words or years to grasp what you're driving at. You are under oath to truth as your personal demon reveals it. When you are writing about life that is all you have to give.

You must subdue the parent in you, the pre-packaged moralizer in you, the disciplinarian or the crank in you – unless it be to isolate those attitudes you did not possess when you were ten or twelve or fourteen. Those attitudes are the eggs of the cuckoo.

If you are to recreate childhood with integrity, you have to *identify* all the way, no matter how passionately grown-ups are going to accuse you of selling out on adult authority or dignity. If you really *are* concerned about those values you are in the wrong vocation – or you are still immature as a writer. It is remarkable how quickly routine adult viewpoints set in once the sobering achievement of parenthood has been attained. Accepted viewpoints need not necessarily be right, yet every day some wild lad changes from a harem-scarem (in the proper sense of the meaning) to a righteous citizen and adds sonorously to the parental clamour.

To reach children in the dimension I am talking about, I believe you must regenerate your child-mind and see the world in that old-time emotional brilliance that used to leave you all-of-a-tremble. If you break through into it – what an adventure waits. When you enter into the world again as a child, when you make this emotional leap, there are no longer real inhibitions or real prohibitions to fence you out or hold you off, there is no longer a problem of what to write about or how to handle it. It is all there, waiting to be explored. You have your adult skills to enable you to sort things out, added to the exhilaration of a ten- or twelve- or fourteen-year-old heartbeat. Instinctively you know whether your theme is in key or flat. That it is still possible to make mistakes simply adds to the zest.

Can method be defined?

In literature can there be a method? Can there be an ordered approach? I suspect that once rules are made or adopted or obeyed, it becomes a process, not a creation. It can be an elegant process and an elegant result, but does it carry the distinction or the style or the poise of an original unique in itself? Yet what is a human being but a miracle of unique variation within a given frame? I am arguing against myself. I do not know whether there is method or not.

One distinguished friend of mine claims that he sees it all, then puts it down, as Mozart (I am told) used to do. The magnitude of this intelligence crushes me. Dare I confess that my creative spirit (if it is to be dignified by the classification) stretches and strives and struggles? The theme is always there, dormant or growing imperceptibly since the dawn of awareness, I guess. The main theme. The lead theme. The broadest concept of what the book is to be about in the broadest possible terms, yet sometimes it is so feeble that it lies all but lost beneath what I finish up with. I am not meticulous or fussy or impatient at the beginning, even if the whole thing looks suspiciously like a puff of wind. I find that building a book is much like building a wall; I manage best a brick at a time. But there is a difference. The wall you finish up with often resembles closely the wall you originally had in mind. The book you finish up with may come as a staggering surprise.

I choose my characters and to this group of people rarely add. Those I glimpse first of all usually see me through to the end. Almost always they grow from reality, from adults I know pictured as children, or actual children about me now or known way back. They *do* grow in the book, they become different in the book. Some are born out of fragments, fragments of other people, fragments of myself, and create themselves, create their own lives. Even a name has generating power, so I know the meanings of names or can refer to their meanings in appropriate dictionaries. This can take days, the choosing and naming of characters, with care, with anticipation, with expectation, even with excitement.

I select the scene. (These initial steps are deliberate steps.) Is it to happen in a city, or a country town, on a mountain, beside the sea, down a hole, up a tree? The pleasurable

63

toying with alternatives. Scene influences character. Bill under tension is different from Bill at ease. Jane on a mountain is not the same as Jane beside the sea. Fascinating.

My book is still a mystery, an unexplored land. It can be anything of a thousand million things; I think one can reasonably say a thousand million books are out there, waiting to be found. But little by little, by luxuriously day-dreaming, I am narrowing the choice down; more often than not drawing closer unawares to the story that will invite me in this time. Twelve hours a day it might hold me for a week or two weeks or more, just looking for the door, with little to show, but I have learnt not to rush, not to push hard. Better to relax, to enjoy myself, slowly swinging my chair, deleting all uninviting possibilities, or grossly improper ones (that can happen, you know), discarding all stupidities and irrationalities, until the moment is there. "Eureka." The door! It opens. A mood, a word, a certainty that from *here* I go on into the unknown, that inexhaustible source of originalities from out of which comes excitement that I wish all could enjoy. The unknown is a word ahead of me all the time, word by word I move out into it, a patient, wondering, questing exploration. A contemplation of the word. This might begin to sound a bit precious. In practice it is not. It is an adventure.

Why are so many writers in a hurry? Out of haste comes mediocrity, comes the cliché, comes the predictable situation and word, comes the usual old story. I know there are exceptions, I know there are times when the fire burns brightly and furiously, but it is uncommon for these times to be built in significant or satisfying terms upon other than the pure excitement of preparatory meditation and considered choice. To writers who ask me, I say, "Give yourself a chance. Allow your story to find its way. Discover your story day by day. Exercise your control of it by rejecting the false. For every right way there are innumerable wrong ways. Your quality as a writer depends upon your talent for making choices." Discovering a good story day by day is an enormous joy. It is like living another life.

64

Everything you have is committed, your entire intellectual and emotional and spiritual resources.

Out of this contemplative approach comes the wisdom that surprises you, all the themes that build your book, the innumerable themes that arise unexpectedly, the mood, the tone, the depth, the breadth, the humanity – all these qualities are born from contemplation of your own word. Not from reflections of what others have done, not from great poetry or great prose sub-consciously recalled, not borrowed, not stolen, not strayed in because the fence was down.

As a writer I have no recognizable scale against which to judge, and impose none, except the rhythms of the Bible, the King James, sown during far-away hearings of childhood when the ground-work was done, rhythms from the pulpit, rhythms from readings at home. The back pew with my mother and father and younger brother was my college, old-time non-conformist preachers were my lecturers, the only serious lecturers I have ever known. There was a depression and my father died and there was work to be done. At just fourteen years of age school was gone, suddenly, in a day. I went to school in the morning; at about eleven a.m. I was called away.

Fulfilment is not the acclaim. Fulfilment is the work as it goes, as it leaves you at the end of a long day, or a long year, trembling, glowing, warm.

5 Real Adventure Belongs to Us

The May Hill Arbuthnot Honor Lecture, 1974,
read at the University of Washington, Seattle, on
10 May 1974. Published in *Top of the News*
(journal of the Children's Services Division of the
American Library Association) June 1974 – ©
Copyright American Library Association.

It is a development of many talks given over
about ten years, its most immediate progenitor
being an off-the-cuff address delivered at the
University of Sydney on 8 July 1972. A half-hour
abridgement was broadcast by the Australian
Broadcasting Commission to celebrate Australian
Children's Book Week in 1972.

The version printed here closely follows the
Arbuthnot lecture but includes extra material.

In this chapter I hope to relate the simple tale of a boy who
searched the world for a book to read and found it in a moment
on a mountain. This does not mean it is a tale for children,
though dreaming up stories for children to read is the labour
of my life. There is no compulsion of course, either way, that I
should write or that children should read. Perhaps no book of
mine ever has been genuinely read by a child – I accept my
reassurances on trust – even if I have letters expressing the delight of this child, the doubt of that child, the perceptive criticism
of a few, and occasionally the compliment of a request for photographs, please, for the classroom gallery, by return of mail: "It's
not that we go for your books much, Mr Southall, but we're
collecting photographs of things. Last week it was old steam
engines. This week it's you."

It is a truth, I have never witnessed with my own eyes any
child, freely, in his own time, without compulsion – except one

adoring daughter – actually at it. (And the one in the daughter's lap was about herself.) Once, in a bookshop, I stood behind a likely-looking lad at the brink of decision, *had his hands on a Southall*, but changed his mind and bought *Zip Magee and the Mud Monster* or something of the kind. One day I shall sit in a railway carriage and it'll happen. Out of the pocket of someone's jeans shall come a dog-eared copy of a familiar masterpiece and this kid will curl up in the corner with it and there it will be. Perhaps I'll lean across and tap him on the arm. "Do you really like it? What do you really think of it, hey?" And he'll look up, and shift his gum to the other cheek. "It's for kids, Dad. What's it to you? You'd never understand."

Perhaps I wouldn't. As the man I am without the pen in my hand, perhaps I wouldn't.

Amongst the letters (I risk the parody the confession invites), are those that begin, "Dear Ivan". Not *Dear Sir* or *Dear Mr So-and-So*. From children who communicate; from others who ask, "Why is it so? What am I to do? I know you'll know what I mean." Turning to me as if I were a brother a little older, far enough ahead to have gained a little wisdom, but close enough to touch, someone in whom a confidence is safe; not knowing me as I am, a grandfather many years and a thousand miles or ten thousand miles removed. They picture me as Josh or Michael or Max or Matt – or Frances or Jan or Abigail. Are they victims of a delusion? Or am I? There are grown-ups who say, "Southall doesn't write for kids; he writes about them to exorcize his hang-ups."

I begin my tale knowing I cannot bring you to a reasonable end. Is there ever an end? Is any answer permanent? Is any conclusion final? Ideas and men grow only through change.

Books were not easy to come by when I was a lad. I lived at the fringe of an Australian city where settled suburbs lost definition, and orchards and horse paddocks and bushland began. We had patches in our pants, not because it was the "in-thing", but because bare skin would have bloomed otherwise. There were magpies warbling in the morning and kookaburras laughing and long queues of unemployed. We had heard of wireless sets that spoke out loud, but did not own one. Nor did anyone else we knew.

Money went for food, mainly, in our kind of world. Public money, what there was of it, went for bridges and roads and drains. It was a developing country and disastrously depressed and there were no libraries for children. I used to walk a mile or so to the library to borrow books for my parents. There wasn't a book in the place for a kid to take away, that anyone told me about, or that I can recall. Libraries were for grown-ups. For real people. You know?

Kids read penny comics – full of stories, not pictures – printed in England about three months earlier. For us in the Antipodes they were always out of date and out of season and all the competitions and free privilege offers had long before closed. No Australian story comic ever lasted more than an issue or two. If it were of Australian origin everyone supposed – from a century or more of indoctrination – that it would have to be second-rate and because of this conditioning it usually was. The only enduring Australian comics I can remember were given away as supplements inside newspapers. They never had to stand up unsupported, to the brunt of the market-place. Good things, that parents would buy for you, came from England, and we were expected to accept this as natural, and we did accept it, although everything was different and alien and bore little resemblance to the life we lived at the bottom of the world. Hence we grew up in a kind of limbo, as second- or third-class English children, displaced, out of context, out of tune, deep down doubting the rightness of being where we were.

In the stories we read, English children played in the snow at Christmas time; we had never seen snow and Christmas was a hundred in the shade. English children played soccer; we knew nothing of the game. English children went to boarding schools; what on earth were they? These things would not have mattered if it had been possible to identify – there *is* a universal language greater than these differences, but our stories missed it somehow. Not for a moment do I suggest that these problems hung over us daily like doom, but they took something away from our childhood and insidiously affected eventual adult life.

The English were always the goodies, the Germans were bad, the Americans were called Yanks and made a lot of noise. Australia never earned a mention except as the wilderness to which profligate cousins were sent and out of which lost uncles came. To be Australian in the old British Empire was to be born with a raging inferiority complex (millions of those Australians are alive today), and national life at the adult level was a fierce struggle to prove to the English that at least we could beat them at games. At everything else they were supreme and frequently let us know, by descending upon us out of Heaven as the "ultimate experts" upon all things, as the "final authorities" to whom all matters were referred; even, God help us, to judge our dog shows.

From our English comics we learnt the fundamental truths of life: for instance, people with yellow skins were inscrutable and cunning, people with brown skins were childlike and apt to run amok, people with black skins were savages, but, if tamed, made useful carriers of heavy loads on great expeditions of discovery conducted by Englishmen. It was in order for black people to be pictured without clothes; after all, they didn't know what clothes were and didn't *count*, somehow. But white nudity was unimaginable, except in solid marble or in ill-lit galleries on very old paintings. The white body was so sacred it was not proper to look at your own.

Childhood in the twenties and thirties was a kind of comic culture, for us an alien culture denying us our own, built upon the products of overworked hack writers which kids bought and sold and traded and exchanged until they were tattered beyond further use, until the print from excessive reading practically faded from the page. These comics were imbued with blunt simplicities (the writers had no time for subtleties), with unquestioning loyalty to God and the British Throne, with the absolute morality of good or bad, bravery or cowardice, truth or falsehood, adventure or sloth, British or non-British. Death for God and King – they were synonymous and interchangeable – was the ultimate virtue.

Books for children, conceived with artistic integrity and emotional honesty and *soul*, to help balance this lop-sided culture, were not to be found, largely, I suppose, because writers had been formed in the same mould, taught not to think but to believe, unless by uncommon virtue of intellectual merit or by fortunate accident of birth they were of the élite. Education for the élite functioned in another dimension. Those liberated spirits, or the brave ones, or the honest ones, were not to be found among the writers who spoke directly to my generation. I never came to hear of them while I was a child. The voices of the brave did not get through to the boy or girl sitting up in bed reading the comics of forty or fifty or more years ago. This is not to imply that the old British world gone was all bad. How absurd that would be, but for some, as their literature reveals, it was a form of Utopia where they lived and loved in fine houses and exercised their talents at civilized leisure, while masses of the population *underneath* existed on the breadline, their status little better than serfdom. For us, the colonials, despite our inferiority complexes, we did know where we had come from and where we were going; God was in his Heaven, the King was on his Throne, and we believed. To live in the sun was enough. To be British was enough. What greater birthright for anyone could there be?

Libraries for children, those years ago, from which some sort of choice could be made, had not reached the bottom of the world. There was a library – that is what it was called – on the lower shelf of a cupboard at school, the cupboard where the chalk dusters were put away. Open the door and sneeze. Take a book home and sneeze. I sneeze now, out of respect, as I write it down. Books bound in purples and golds and adorned with flowers and scrolls, bestowed upon the school by someone's grandmother cleaning up a room; books published about the turn of the century in England of course, designed specifically to improve, with titles like *Daniel's Good Deed* by Richard Righteous and *The Best Girl in Form Four* by Patience Virtue. Didn't impress me much, I fear.

I was handling all the improvement I needed. Used to leave home on Sunday mornings at 9.30 for Junior Christian Endeavour. Used to stay on for 11 o'clock family worship. Used to go back for Sunday School at 2.30 p.m. More often than not was there again with my parents for evening service at 7.00. Kept me off the streets – for sure!

I had an ambition as a lad to be steward on the church door. The steward met your family on the steps, issued hymns books to those old enough to read and trustworthy enough not to make paper darts out of loose pages for aiming at the choir, and escorted you with minor ceremony to your pew. At half-time he brought the plate to collect the pennies, then, quietly closing behind him the swing doors, retired to the porch to "keep an eye on things" while everyone else inside enjoyed the sermon. The older I became the better sense it made. When I grew up I would be the steward and sit outside.

The bench that bore the imprint of the steward's backside was, in fact, the lid of a box as long as the breadth of the porch; underneath it, hiding there, was the Sunday School Library. This consisted largely of books, multiple copies I must suppose, written by Arthur Mee, all of which, I am reasonably sure, were designed to improve. I can recall with something approaching totality those areas of my childhood I concentrate upon. I have concentrated hard upon books by Arthur Mee. Nothing stirs. The curtain remains down. Does this mean I was a Philistine, that I never read one through?

There was another source of books; oh, a rich source for the village genius. Every year the same kid was dux of the class at school and won the big prize, a book with lots of pages in it, along with the history prize, the geography prize, the arithmetic prize, the scripture prize. You name it; what ever it was he got it. That's what made him dux. Winston was his name.

Every time I drew near him I felt myself to be in the presence of the elect. If he spoke to me I'd start stammering.

In the Third Grade I fell in love with Miss James. It was not that she was a ravishing beauty (I am sure she was not), but she was *nice*. Every other boy in the class fell in love with her too. Winston as well, I suppose, unless elementary responses were beneath his plane. One of the saddest hours of my young life came on the last school day of that year, 1929, because we were going up next year, all of us except her; we were leaving our beloved teacher behind. The immensity of these tragedies when you're eight years old, going on nine. The immensity of them at any age.

Half-way through the summer holidays a removal van came up our street and stopped at the empty house opposite ours. Guess who got down? Guess who opened the squeaky iron gate and walked up the path with the key? My love. It was she.

First day of the new school year there was I, at 8.40, tapping at her door. "Hullo, Miss James," I said, looking way up there, worshipping her, "may I carry your case to school? Please."

Where did the courage come from? A borrowing from later years? Imagine my joy when she agreed and try to picture the magnitude of my bliss (no other word) when I learnt she was going up with us into Grade Four. Think of her bliss, too. She had all of us for another year.

Every morning at 8.40, excluding a one-month break for measles, there was I proudly bearing her case away, walking beside her, adoring her, for a whole year. That December I won my only school prize. The Progress Prize. For exactly what I am not sure. I have it still, chosen by her, *Tony's Desert Island* by Enid Leale.

One other source of books was open; one requirement only needed by the healthy child to get his hands on them – sainthood.

Sunday School prize-giving came round once a year. To be in at the kill you were required to sustain over a period of fifty-two successive weeks the kind of self-discipline and self-denial that makes heroes. Each Sunday Southall arrived at 2.30 p.m, dead on time, wet or fine, fit or all but totally incapacitated, catechism word perfect, text known to the last dot over the last "i", wearing his neatest home-mades and his most charming manner. Five marks you gained for an impeccable performance in all departments, one mark each for attendance, punctuality, behaviour, catechism, and text. I was impeccable.

Holidays were a problem if you were lucky enough to get them. Sunday School never went into recess. You could always catch up on catechisms and texts, but if you did not attend, for any reason, even banishment to an infectious diseases hospital, you lost your attendance mark, your punctuality mark, and your behaviour mark. The system was incorruptible, beyond concession to human weakness or resort to human compassion. Every week of absence sent you three marks more down the drain. For holidays I dared visit no one but my Great Aunt Susan in the country, despite my enormous fear of snakes and my loathing of the Throne Room at the bottom of the garden.

Great Aunt Susan was the most daunting, the most exciting, the most eccentric, the most magnificent, the most loved adult of my boyhood outside my own home. She lived in the land of wooden trestle bridges and cow-pats and asparagus and mine shafts and pine trees and empty buildings and strong children. From Auntie Susie's Sunday School class I was able to secure those vital marks firmly initialled on an official card as evidence beyond dispute of my unbroken endeavour.

Year in, year out, until I was sixteen, I sustained this feat to win each March the prize, that I might have a book of my own, that I might have a book to possess. I have them still, and all but two, of strong religious content (a sinking disappointment *they* were, and put aside with a sense of having been betrayed), are adventure stories set in exotic climes. The only books for a boy to read I ever really saw, the only ones I ever really read – over and over and over again – yet it is not hindsight to observe that something always was missing, the *possibility* of believable identification. In any situation I read about I could see myself only by suspending belief in myself. I would not have put it into those words at the time, but I knew.

The hero, inevitably, would be fair-haired, blue-eyed, English, incredibly brave, incredibly good, incredibly handsome, clean-cut, wholesome, masculine, modest, brilliant, called Nigel. Nigel is dux of his class, captain of the cricket team, a total abstainer from cigarettes, swearing, girls, and all other evil. In the books I read only bounders smoked cigarettes behind the rose bushes, only cads and sissies associated with girls of any kind, except mothers, sisters and aunts. In all honesty, despite my huge religious experience and my public face of shining innocence, there was always the certainty that my only possible relationship had to be with the cads, the bounders, and the cowards.

Nigel's mother of sacred memory has been dead three years, and his father, Professor Armstrong-Manly, has vanished in darkest Africa. There, at the moment of discovery of a lost city lodged in the interior walls of a once-dormant but now active volcano, deserted by his faithless carriers, he has slipped from his exploration of the rim, that knife-edged bit that goes around the top where one must balance with great care, if one is an English professor in an adventure story for boys. Down he has slipped to lie trapped on a ledge fifty feet below, out of reach of the top, out of sight, an appalling plight. But he survives, fed by friendly apes on breadfruit and coconut milk, kept in good heart by diamonds brought daily by the apes from the lost city, and warmed at night by the gentle bubbling of the lava far below. At length, he teaches Yang You-tang, king of the apes, to carry a message bottle to the great river that sweeps down to the sea. Months later the bottle is swept ashore at Land's End, there to be found by fifteen-year-old Tom Sykes, an honest apprentice coalminer who has just ridden a bicycle from Yorkshire to prove that coalmining is good for you. Tom leaps back on his bicycle and rides to Manly Manor to deliver the bottle into Nigel's hands.

"Come at once," the note says, giving the map co-ordinates in code, "I am in terrible danger. The volcano must erupt at any moment. Beware of a tall man with a black eye-patch and a guttural accent. Signed, Professor Armstrong-Manly, your long-lost father."

"My goodness," Nigel exclaims, "I must sail for darkest Africa without delay. Come with me, good Tom. Be my faithful friend and who can tell what your reward may be."

"To the death," Tom vows.

Hastily packing his portmanteau and placing in his left breast pocket a photograph of his mother and in his right breast pocket a leather-bound edition of the Holy Scriptures, Nigel begins his epic journey. Thanks to sharp-eyed, loyal Tom, a man with a black eye-patch is eluded on the boat train and again at Southampton as they board the SS *Windsor Castle*. The voyage to darkest Africa is a battle of wits against treacherous Chinese crewmen in the pay of Black Patch, who travels incognito, blasphemously disguised as a Lutheran missionary.

Meanwhile, back at the volcano, Professor Armstrong-Manly has lain trapped on the ledge these past two years and is but a husk of his former self, withered by the fierce equatorial sun and by gusts of heat rising from the evil depths of bubbling lava, weary unto death of breadfruit and coconuts, no longer able when conscious to recall the English tongue, though when delirious crying his son's name in a loud voice, which issues eerily on still nights from the crater, giving rise along the Congo to the legend that the volcano is haunted.

Nigel and Tom, fighting their way into darkest Africa, forever fearful their faint-hearted carriers may desert, attacked by lions and pygmies with blow-pipes, trailed by Black Patch despite every desperate manoeuvre to mislead him, come at last to the volcano from which rises smoke and sulphur fumes and cries of Nigel's name.

The earth shakes. Sounds like thunder roll in the heavens. A major eruption is imminent. As foretold in ancient writings, hundreds of apes abandon the lost city and rush blindly into the night never to be seen again. The faithless carriers flee to their deaths, falling into fissures, drowning in rivers, eaten by tigers, strangled by boa constrictors. Patch appears at the jungle fringe, revolver in hand.

"Courage, Tom," cries Nigel, and together they scale the slope, Patch after them shooting wildly, as great boulders shaken by earth tremors break loose. Nigel races along the crater rim shouting, "Father, Father, it is I," while Tom engages Patch in hand-to-hand combat. From his portmanteau Nigel takes a fifty-foot length of rope, slaps the grappling hook over the lip of the crater, shins down into the blistering heat and suffocating sulphurous gases, throws his father across his shoulders and climbs the rope again as it begins to burn spontaneously in his grasp. Patch, screaming his guttural last, is overcome by Tom, and drops from the lip a great depth into the fiery pit. The heroes reach a cave by the river as the volcano blows up and the lost city is destroyed forever. The professor, already growing stronger, shows them a bulging bag of diamonds, a million pounds worth of diamonds. "All thanks to loyal Tom," declares Nigel. So Tom is given a diamond of his very own and a job for life in the kitchen at Manly Manor.

How does a run-of-the-mill colonial kid, or anyone else for that matter, identify with characters like Nigel? Shinning up and down ropes rescuing fathers from volcanoes, when you're not *allowed* to climb a ladder and the only time you climb a tree it takes half-a-day to get down again because of vertigo?

So brave, so noble, so true, so strong, so clever, so generous, so pure, so rich, so English, when you're a skinny streak of thirteen selling newspapers at the railway gates after school to help the family, handing over your earnings at the end of the week, though hoping to fiddle a penny on the side to buy a hot potato cake, only passing your exams when you can cheat a bit, worried by strange things happening in your body and to your thoughts that no one grown-up will tell you about, except to infer in every possible way that sexuality in a boy is dirty and less than human, sure you're a coward because you're scared of tough kids and high trees and deep holes and all that dying stuff that goes with wars, though marching off to war, cheered and adored by all the girls (*because* you're marching off to war) and singing as you go because you're so happy about it, is being British to the core.

Did you ever read about a completely believable boy or girl who spoke your language and thought your thoughts and had your problems and experienced your fears and was sometimes bad or stupid or troubled or irritable or sexy or frightened half to death, but could be a nice kid too? If you were an Australian in my day I am all but certain you could not. If you were an ordinary working-class English child, I am sure you were not much better served, *and* for reasons that might have been more immediately disturbing. If you were American at least you had librarians who liked children, and you did have, even then, wonderful libraries and there were books to borrow, though whether their authors faced life or ran from it or distorted it I am unable to say; I was down under, too far away to know, hanging into space by my feet, my brain addled by English super-heroes.

There were movies, of course, to add variety to the culture, if you could nag the money out of Mum once in a while or slip in the side door at interval time, but they didn't count much. They were American, so there was no need to believe them. You cheered the serial like mad, Buck Jones and Tom Mix and all the rest, but they were grown-up characters and identifying with them never came into it, and when you went outside into fierce daylight you left them behind you, behind the door, in the house of make-believe.

Your books and story comics were different. They were at home under the pillow. Open them, any time, and the English public schoolboy hero was inside. The motive at the source, if motive came into it, was to present what were supposed to be high ideals and high principles, to encourage you to be big and brave and bold for God and King and Empire (God and Empire also being interchangeable, with blasphemy embracing all three), and to prepare you to die to preserve the status-quo, though your personal stake in the status-quo might best be described as *pathetic*. If you were insensitive, the aims were generally achieved. If you were sensitive, you were left to carry the humiliating truth of your weakness, whilst forming wholly misleading ideas about the true nature of your contemporaries and of real living English public schoolboys.

I know this is a simplification. I know many factors in depths of time and history contributed. All were related, I believe, but I am reluctant to pursue them, because I am by no means certain where I may end up. Perhaps a man should keep a couple of heaps of sand. Instead, please allow me to jump to conclusions.

If, over a long period, you never hear the other side of an argument or a proposition, you don't know about it.

If, over a long period, you are taught that your mother country and its allies are honourable and of noble intention and others are dishonourable and selfishly motivated, it would be surprising if you did not accept it.

If, over a long period, you are taught by word and inference in church and school and everywhere else, to feel sorry for people with skins of a different colour, not because their rights as human beings are more greatly eroded than your own, but *because* their skins are different, can you be judged for false attitudes?

If, over a long period, no one gives you good books and you can neither borrow them nor buy them and you do not know they exist, how are you to be influenced by their values? How are they to add richness and understanding to your experience if they are not accessible? And the great literature compulsorily administered like medicine at school speaks a language the ordinary child finds difficult to understand, and the fact that it *is* taught at school, sometimes clumsily, alienates it from your spirit perhaps for all time.

A proportion of the human race doesn't give a damn about anything but the more obvious appetites, I know that; some people never have raised their eyes and are not likely to; but man has come to where he is, culturally as distinct from materially, because sensitive people have cared; or have accepted a truth because they have confronted it face to face; or have been compelled to search for it because of inner disquiet; or instinctively, have created it out of their own souls, sometimes unawares, sometimes despite themselves, and have been able to express it in the language of their day.

Simply from looking at myself as a boy and being aware of effects, I know that the words children read for recreation are of prodigious importance. No matter how you regard this material, as an opportunity to present life to children honestly, without sentimentality or intentional bias, without denying man's humanity or glorifying it or belittling it – or whether you see it as an opportunity to distort or indoctrinate or pervert or enslave – the degree of influence is not something you can put a measure on. The ultimate influence, on the course of adult taste alone, may well be permanent unless the process is reversed by firm re-education.

If you raise a dozen children or a million children or ten million children on falsehoods and phonies and trivialities – through your own ignorance or indifference or deliberate intention – you end up with a substantial number of grown persons who need to be sustained by lies and illusions and cheap sentimentalities because they cannot live with truth or be bothered by the effort of comprehension art demands. Switch on the box and there it is to see. In terms of human wastage you dare not even think about it. Man bent upon poisoning himself.

At fourteen I was out working full-time and never encountered literature in an atmosphere or situation where it had a chance with me or I had a chance with it. As a youth, life was largely work at my trade as a process engraver and attending night school to learn my trade and a frantic spare-time endeavour to appease the fever to write. This was usually done against the clock as if tomorrow I were to die and a million things were to be written down first. But a million things were

79

not to be written down except the most trivial absurdities. There was nothing else I knew and my own experience was unsuitable as raw material to draw upon. I had done nothing brave or noble or exciting. I had done nothing but grow up, ten thousand miles from practically everywhere.

I wrote in clichés throughout my youth as I had read throughout my boyhood – of swashbuckling deeds in darkest Africa or up the Amazon, of non-stop cliff-hanging physical adventure in which the baddies spoke with guttural accents and the savages were black or brown and the cunning heathens were yellow. Putting into effect my long and thorough briefing. There was nothing else I knew, except the Bible. It, too, was full of super heroes and hostility between races and high and bloodthirsty adventure. There were other levels in the Bible, and I knew them intimately, but they were not for writing about if you were a boy. Perhaps for thinking about in an un-questioning way, but not for proclaiming in the world where a boy lived. The boy, even such a short while ago, was the warrior in training, was the fodder for the gun, from the day he focused on his mother's smile. The gentler parts of the Bible were for girls: even the lessons in Sunday School were differently oriented and differently directed. Boys went for David and Goliath, and Joshua and Jericho, and Samson and the ass's jawbone, and Moses and the drowned Egyptians, and Meshach, Shadrach and Abednego. And a thousand more like them . . . Wonderful stories . . . Of violence and destruction and hatred and indiscriminate *judgement*. Is the struggle lost at the source before we begin?

My turn came. The boy frightened in a tree, the boy who had never hurt a friend or an enemy with his hands, learned to accept the thunder of flying-boat engines in his ears and the warring world of sea and space into which he flew many times. Fear was a part of every day, none more total than on the night he fulfilled and justified his life-long briefing. An explosion of violence in the air and on the Atlantic directed by me. So I was decorated for qualities I admired in others but found wanting in myself. I was given a ribbon to wear under my wings and a silver cross in a leather case that I have kept along with *Tony's Desert Island* by Enid Leale.

How was it that a coward came to wear a hero's badge? Or had I been misinformed? Was fear not cowardice? Was fear-sickness not cowardly either? The sickness that shook you, that possessed you, that filled you with dread of dying so young, so soon. Were there no such people as the heroes of my indoctrination? Were decorated men scared and ordinary like me? Was being brave – for lack of a better word – something a frightened lad could be?

I did not allow those improper thoughts to be publicly viewed. I held up my head and played the hero with the self-effacing manner best suited to the role, but was never over-reluctant to go without my coat that the glory of my jacket might be seen. True, I was a nice young fellow and didn't blatantly boast or brag or grossly misbehave, but I missed a chance to mature before my time. I simply joined the club, but should have baled out from conformity then and there. So for fifteen more years in my series of books for boys I went on perpetuating the myths of my growing years.

Simon Black was my hero, developed from stories I had written in adolescence. He was the first character I came up with after I set out twenty-seven years ago to take on the world, abandoning my trade and what security it gave me. Cutting adrift. Going it alone. Both courageous and foolish, I suppose, in a country and at a time when professional writers earning a living from books were numbered on a couple of fingers of one hand. But I retreated into my childhood; for defence or some slight security, I imagine; not into the depths of my childhood, but into its superficialities and indoctrinations.

Simon, this character of mine, emerged from his pre-war beginnings to become a decorated air force officer, a former flying-boat pilot who had flown in the Battle of the Atlantic, brown-eyed, black-haired, lean, six feet tall, Australian, modest, incredibly good, incredibly clever, incredibly brave, incredibly handsome – me. The super me. Same person, of course, as the super you.

Nothing was too difficult for Simon. Getting to Mars back in 1952 might have been tricky, but he made it in the end in a spaceship designed in his spare time, between rushing all over the earth solving problems beyond the wit of presidents and kings and the capacity of armies. It is fair to point out that I did not write these stories to cash in, they were not an exploitation – my wife and young family quietly starved along with me – nor did I write deliberately to pervert or subvert or indoctrinate or perpetuate the status-quo, any more than did the generation of writers before me. Like them, I thought it was the proper and only thing to do. And I was much too busy trying to scrape together a living, working twelve to fifteen hours a day, to waste time reading what my more distinguished contemporaries were writing – an ignorance that continues until now.

Each day, whether the book on hand was for children or for adults, the attitude of mind was the same – a strenuous search for bigger and bolder and more breathtaking deeds. Talk about racking my brain. Talk about stretching every winning post to a mile. Used to wear myself out from the stress and strain. Used to stagger off to bed emotionally mangled, at the absolute and despairing end of invention. Next morning, with some fresh absurdity, off I'd go. The agony was the professional pride part of it – the making up of situations *different* from all those situations I had absorbed as a boy.

I knew something was wrong, as I had always known something was wrong, even when I used only to read the stuff, long before I started writing my own. But in my own life nothing but the war was worth drawing from. Nothing else had happened to me and I was much too poor and under-confident and insecure to risk earning time on literary experiment – *if* it had occurred to me as a reasonable possibility. I didn't want to be a hack all my life, but I knew my limitations. There were people who had told me: "Forget the great novel, Ivan. It's not you."

Wrote a comic strip once, for a woman's magazine. That was

more my class. Only regular income we saw in years, except for bits picked up from labouring here and there. We stepped lightly for a while; I believe my wife owned a second pair of shoes; but a new editor came along and policies changed and our strip disappeared. No protests. No deputations to the new editor to convict him of gross stupidity. You would have thought one kid somewhere would have raised a cry. But no. Every newspaper you opened, every weekly magazine, had its strip or its several strips or its dozen strips on exactly the same theme. The super-man theme. *Mike Manly* I called mine.

We lived thirty-two miles from town, up the mountains, over the top, and down the other side; a pocket ignored by progress and time. Eight and three-quarters acres of bushland and four acres cleared falling from a pot-holed red earth road to a creek in a fern gully several hundred yards below; all ours; with a clumsy house of rough-sawn timbers then about fifty years old, and tumbledown outbuildings with harness over rails, and leaning chicken pens though the chickens roosted in trees, and a brooder house and incubators worked by kerosene, and spring-tine cultivators and harrows and ploughs rusting outside. $2,400 the lot. We paid $10 down, created a few hundred, and borrowed the balance from a bank manager who said, "My God; you've got the heart of a lion."

Behind us the world stretched eastward out of sight across valleys and forests and mountains and sky and cloud. On autumn mornings the sun came up behind a plateau of mist fifteen miles wide with such brilliance it was more than eye and spirit could stand. The first time I saw it I was overwhelmed and overawed, and cried.

Eucalyptus forest hedged us on the south, tall and dark and sometimes unnerving. I had a "thing" about that piece of forest. It began a hundred yards from the house and I never walked into it. Shout at it and the echo cracked back. For a while I called it *Echo Farm*; but it made my wife nervous. She was just a girl, and English, and sometimes afraid of the strangeness outside her door. So I changed the name.

On the north boundary, a quarter of a mile across paddocks, lived an old man; well, he seemed old to me. Fifty years he had been there, and had pioneered a block when only thirteen. He was so *right* for that hillside. How can such things disappear? A small man, bow-legged, hard, kind, with a body like wire. Cut his wrist once with an axe; the nearest doctor a walk of eight miles. Held himself together with his hand and climbed the hill to his house for aid. When they saw him they fainted – his wife and daughter – out like two corpses on the kitchen floor. So he put the kettle on and boiled water and sterilized a needle and a hair he plucked from the draught horse's tail and stitched himself up again.

Twenty-five years ago – there we began. The city left behind us; all our bridges chopped down. A burnt-out one-fire stove to cook on, a sheet-iron fireplace on wooden stumps to keep out the cold. Termites in the foundations, termites in the walls. A thousand-gallon tank was all the water on hand. Numerous other tanks rusted out with holes stood around. No water on tap from the town supply, though a large reservoir was a mile away. No electricity; candles and lamps with mantles and hissing sounds. No local services provided by the shire except a grader once a year down the road. No sewerage – and no night man to take away the pan. A one-holer fifty feet from the back door, full of spiders and scuttling lizards and pulse-arresting pauses – one was so defenceless there. But we had a bathroom, by name; fourteen feet long and three feet wide – at one time a passage, but made into a room. At the narrow end a tap from the tank outside poked through the wall. The bath was of sheet-iron, huge and old with feet of ball and claw. The water heater was a Malley, a black cylindrical object of sinister appearance – like a depth-charge – one foot wide and three feet tall standing on the floor at the distant end between the bath and the outside wall. All conveniences, as it were, in single file. Getting to the water heater or to the tap or into the bath was rather like negotiating the corridor of a crowded train.

Let me tell you about the Malley: a little funnel on top to

receive water trickled from the tap, and a large sooty hole (a venturi) through which you poke paper and sticks and bark and the burning match. There is a pregnant period – and that is the proper word – then BOOM, you leap back, eyebrows scorched, heart thudding, and the Malley takes charge, BOOM, BOOM, BOOMING in rhythm, belching light and heat and sparks and flame, all but literally jumping up and down, shaking the house, terrifying everyone around not accustomed to the sound. First time my wife fled outside, snatching up our young son on the way, and crept back later to see if I was alive. Then, out of the spout of this marvellous machine, comes a thin, thin stream of scalding hot water, a kind of mystical experience. But you cannot turn it off until the fire dies down and the water runs cold, not an embarrassment unless you have climbed in too soon. There I squatted one night, in the light of a candle-flame, feet drawn up under me at the high end away from the ferocious spout, compromised and anxious and cooking like a crayfish. I could have escaped over the back, I suppose, at the risk of slipping a disc, but made a long forward step to turn the tap on full to flood the heater and the bath with cold, and went out through layers of paint and rust, out through the bottom, and away poured everything into the house.

We were too poor to buy another bath and for four years went without. We used the concrete wash troughs under the plum tree instead. The drill was to half-fill both troughs, put your rear end in one and your feet in the other and pray for solitude. That we bathed like this for four years unobserved I doubt, particularly in the light of the evidence reported by our neighbour's wife. She kept an eye on things when we were not about. "I heard a car come and go," she said, "so I thought you were home. I popped over to say hullo, but I knew it wasn't you. The footprints were not the same."

Several adults were in the house one night, long ago, my mother-in-law among them, conversing with the spirit in the glass. Not really my kind of entertainment – an old English pastime you might have heard about. A load of old rubbish, I thought, while that glass rushed in circles around my table with a message allegedly from my father, dead fifteen years by then, a good man, a gentle man, an impressive man, worn-out at forty-seven from hard work begun when he was eight, and the whole thing troubled me a bit. But the glass persisted and one does not offend the guests. "Ask it questions," they said, so I asked, "How is it I survived the war when every day I was sure I couldn't last?"

"I flew beside you," the glass said.

For pity's sake. What do you do about a thing like that? So I said, "Will I survive as a writer?"

"Yes," the glass spelt out. "Have faith."

My next question was even more out of character. All I wish for the future, then as now, is that it should happen in its own way in its own time, but I asked, "What will I be doing in a month?"

"Digging for gold," the glass spelt out.

"It's stupid," I said, "the whole thing's stupid."

But the glass went on.

There was gold, it said, £60,000 worth (half-a-million dollars in the values of today) at a depth of sixty feet, at the bottom of a shaft sunk sixty years before by Chinese prospectors who had died from misadventure. If I would proceed along a given line for a given distance, then turn left at right angles for forty-two feet, the shaft would be mine.

Next morning my mother-in-law was up at about six. "Come along," she said, "everybody out. Let's find it." Truly, I wanted none of it, but after breakfast we were in the bush with surveyor's tape and compass and blackberry slasher and axe. Getting through that jungle in the required direction took half the day and at precisely the given point, in the midst of rampant blackberries and scrub of fierce growth, I found the shaft. Brimming with water. I swear it.

I was ahead of the others, on my own. Everything went quiet, and from the rear someone called, "Are you all right?"

I was far from all right. I was about to walk away from it, to

86

ignore it, to conceal it, to forget it, but heard myself saying in a voice my family still remembers, "It's here."

We plumbed it to about forty feet, I think, with lengths of half-inch pipe screwed together – that was all the pipe we could handle – and took specimens from the top where rock appeared to have been dropped and hammered them to powder. If it was not gold we were looking at I cannot imagine what else it was. But I took weeks to think this through and turned cautious and stubborn. I viewed it as a choice between the easy way and the hard way, between gold or fulfilment. It might have been something else entirely, but that was how I viewed it. So the bush grew back and the shaft is lost – I made sure of it. Men with bulldozers have come that way since, pushing over trees and changing contours. There are no regrets.

We grew our own food, vegetables in rotation all the year round, a small plot within a tall wire fence; it was that or starve to death. We added eggs and poultry meat, though getting that poor cockerel's head off each Friday night was too much for me in the end. Fourteen years later the survivors and their descendants still staggered about, the oldest domestic fowls on the face of the earth. Even tried farming for a few cash crops. Started off with green peas, but had to plough a half-acre first.

We had Jack, of course, the horse. He came with the place. Largest living thing I ever had communion with. Didn't have any proper fences so he had the run of the estate. Come dinner-time he would thrust his head through the window and whinny for tit-bits, giving my mother-in-law hysterics. On bright nights he used to gallop, thudding, round and round and round the house. Trying to catch him for work was an intellectual feat. As soon as he saw leather he would take off, down the hill and into the bush, kicking up his heels, making explosively vulgar noises from his propulsion end. Hitched him at last to the plough (reading how from a book) and away we went, but not along the contours as hoped. Straight down the hill again at an incredible rate, through all obstacles, and I was lucky to escape with my neck. Next time I hitched him to the spring-tine cultivator and when he tried to bolt I dug the tines in about a foot deep. Between us we tore that half-acre apart and Jack never forgave me.

I planted my peas from the instructions in the home gardening book, though it was not a packet in my hand, but a sack. Seeds two inches apart, rows a foot apart, each pea individually *put*. Took about a week. Up came the crop like a lawn, a wonderful sight. Several times daily I would orbit it admiring the angular effect. Even wrote to the seed company expressing my joy; never had germination like it, I said, which was correct. But it was a long, dry summer. The peas grew stoutly to six inches, turned yellow, and that was that.

I planted lemons and passionfruit for long-term prosperity, three-quarters of an acre of each. Major plantings, as far as I was concerned; every penny spent on nursery stock was crucial; I was so much in debt. "Is it safe to plant them?" I asked the old man next door. "You know, frost and all that?"

"Frost," he said. "Here? You're on an easterly aspect, lad. The sun's warming things for you hours before it's up. That aspect is money in the bank."

In they went, in their beautiful rows, a picture to behold, all measured up, and it was a record cold year to succeed the drought. We even had snow. I rushed frantically from vine to vine and tree to tree covering them with everything I could grab, even the clothes off my back. But not a lemon tree survived. There was never a passionfruit to pick.

Raspberries came next. A quarter of an acre was all I could afford. In stools of three, six feet apart all ways, a sight to see. Everyone grew raspberries so I couldn't go wrong, I couldn't lose, it was the local crop. Along came spring and they burst gloriously into leaf.

One stormy night at half-past two that young woman who was my wife said to me, with mounting shrillness, "It's now, it's now, it's now." So we charged away in our clapped-out baby car, twelve miles through lightning and thunder and mountains and torrential rain for the birth of child Number Two – taking Number One child on to his grandmother, as far as I can recall.

Home at daybreak, on my own, looking around. It was an awful old house, a dreadful old house, that I was trying to rebuild a little at a time as I learnt to use tools. But I was appalled that morning as I looked around; it simply would not do, it could not wait; how could she bring a new baby home?

I bought paint, enough for every room, and worked like a madman, pausing only in the evenings to drive to the hospital and back again. The house didn't look bad after those seven hard days, and I had not told her, for her it was to be a surprise. But for a week I had not viewed the estate, the daily intoxication of the heavy-footed stride, the man of property, thumbs in pockets, glowing with pride. Hadn't seen Jack much either, though he had come up for oats each night, as was his custom, when called. Incredibly voracious creature. Twelve and three-quarter acres to ravage at will, oats thrown in. He liked raspberries too. My quarter-acre was ruined, pulled up by the roots and chewed. Never picked a raspberry either.

Tried half an acre of French beans. They would bring a good price, people said. "Beans do well round here." Seeds four inches apart as recommended in the gardening book, rows eighteen inches apart and straight as railway tracks. Enormous enterprise. The first were germinating before I had time to get the last in. First class season, warm and wet. How those beans shot up. Then the rabbits came. Off I rushed to the old man in wild distress and practically wept.

"Well," he said, "you could fence your beans in, but I know you can't afford that, or you could sit up all night and shoo the rabbits off. . . . I'll tell you," he said, "I'll tell you what. Four gallons of night-soil and six pounds of lime stirred to a paste. Get yourself a brush, lad, and paint every leaf. That'll stop 'em. No rabbit alive'll give them a second look." It's what he said; I give my oath on the Book.

So staunchly I stirred it up, four gallons of night-soil and six pounds of lime, no shortage of ingredients, and took my little brush. Half an acre, up and down the rows, painting every leaf. A nightmare event. And the rabbits still got them, which was just as well I think. And I still don't know whether that old man was serious or not. I was not brave enough, later, to ask.

Every major planting, no matter of what, came to grief.

Farmers are born, I guess.

There were other little things, like foxes among the chickens, and storms smashing windows and sucking out two hundred handwritten manuscripts sheets; never published, never finished, never found. A screaming hurricane at night (called a gale in our latitudes), the house swaying and groaning with bits breaking off, interior walls having just been removed in trepidation by Southall for massive alterations. Panic running loose. Pushing furniture up to the front for defence, rushing round driving nails into everything, hair vertically on end or thereabouts, children and beloved wife cowering under a table at the back of the house . . .

Drought; carrying water in buckets four hundred yards from the old man's well, shade temperatures of up to a hundred and twelve for ten successive days I think, pregnant wife sitting in the creek from seven in the morning until sunset.

Children ill or injured, kicked by Jack, scratched by wild cats, night-time fevers, and no doctor to consult.

Every pet imaginable, silkies and bantams and pigeons and parrots and beautiful dogs and cats and mice and tortoises and white rabbits and guinea pigs and endearing twin billy goats all dying by violence, by inexhaustible bad luck. Those poor kids; heartbreak after heartbreak.

Chimneys ablaze and kerosene stoves blowing up and no telephone to call for help. A screech owl at night, inches from the bedroom window, like a woman under attack. Number One child sitting on a strip of bituminized felt blown from the roof, two deadly snakes coiled underneath. Number Two child, her head caught between floorboard joists under the house: how do you get her out before she chokes? Number Four child, born unwell.

Problems of relationships, of hardship and endless disappointment and monumental misfortune pushing faith to the brink. An uncontrollable forest fire of incredible magnitude in the middle of the night, fire dropping from the heavens and springing up round about as if breaking out of the earth, not knowing if there can be an escape, stunned when the escape happens, drenching rain falling as if arranged by a writer to end a book.

The house finished at last, after fourteen years, an environment made of materials on hand without spending money to achieve an effect, having to give it all up from sheer impoverishment. Nothing to write about either, except swashbuckling stories for boys strenuously invented, set in far-off distant places, and documentary books for adults about larger-than-life adventure arduously researched, one's own experience simply not presenting itself as worth thinking about.

A journalist called, a very good journalist who had reviewed me twice, favourably; each a book for adults. I assumed he had come to talk about my work; I mean, what else? I had written by then about twenty-five books and was pleased that he felt they were worthy of general comment. Later, reading him through, it seemed he was more interested in the life I lived than in the work I produced. I was surprised and embarrassed. I was not obsessed by modesty, but regarded myself as an observer, not as a doer, as a failure in a practical sense. For years I had felt the need to *live* creatively and regretted that I had not taken more positive steps. I heard it said of me in those days by a local gossip that I was a lay-about who didn't know what work meant. I had bristled – what man working eighty hours a week would not? – but I had not gone after her with a stick. Had she been rude about my books I would have jumped up and down on the spot.

I am perturbed at the depths of my indoctrination, at what it accomplished.

I was not dull; I was able to do things for myself and for others, able to lead and speak publicly to some effect without borrowing thoughts or quotations or opinions, but in the context of my greatest endeavour, my work, I remained blind and limp and lame. I observe there is no need to wait for Big-Brother-Watching. Has there ever been a time he has not been with us – or against us – or in us? Every voice that raises itself where children listen should look inwards, should go witch-hunting inwards, should know that the enemy has been planted within himself.

Where does awakening begin? I questioned earlier whether anything has an end. I equally doubt that anything has a beginning. Beginnings and endings are conventions of language. The specific moment that may be said to be the birth of an idea or a book or a change is too subtle to be defined by us. I was taught as a child that Creation is infinite, neither beginning nor ending, I am certain at this moment I was not misinformed. Yet there are opportunities, there are crests of clarity that mark moments of revelation, there are sources that become apparent when one is nudged. I have, in this chapter, passed in part across the origins of every book I am happy to own, as well as a few I would be happy to forget. They are all there; the characters, the situations, the conflict, the development; all are there. If you have detected one or two, you are out in front – I needed *years* to see them for myself. Within the same words lie originating parts of other books still to be discovered. Each discovery made and each book written is part of the last and part of the next.

The major crest of clarity, for me, came one wet Sunday fifteen years back. It is as close to a beginning as I know. My brother and his wife had added their children to ours rushing about the house. By half-past five I was wearing thin and out of a head throbbing from noise said to my brother, "What would happen to these kids if we were not here to pick up the bits, say, for a year or a month – or even a week? What would happen if they were left?"

"They'd die," he said.

They'd die?

Left to fend for themselves in a world without adults, they'd die? Or would they? Super kids would have no problems, but ordinary kids, real kids, a group of kids like ours, as we used to be ourselves, would confront all the hazards and all the wonders of being alive.

Oh, the obvious truth so long in the coming.

Real adventure cannot happen to super heroes; by nature super heroes would have to be insensitive to it; real adventure belongs to us. Being ordinary and inept are acceptable qualities, they give meaning to achievement. There must be contrasts within oneself. One must know weakness to know strength. One must be foolish to be wise. One must be scared to be brave. Adventure is simply experience; the mistakes often enough meaning more than the successes.

I had come to my crest, unexpectedly, on a wet Sunday, or was it a door that fell ajar and I was ready to slip a foot through?

"Write it," something said to me. Clearly said and clearly heard. "You know what, boy; get down to it and write it. It's time that kid who thought he was a coward had a book to read."

6 Children's Literature and Adult Literature: Is There a Boundary?

First delivered on 12 March 1974. A lecture prepared for Writer's Week, a segment of the Adelaide Festival of Arts.

The subject is not of my own making. It came pre-packaged, untouched by human hand as it were, typed bravely – or was it hopefully? – across the invitation:

> *Is there really a boundary between*
> *children's literature and adult literature?*

So I sat and thought about it. I do a lot of sitting and thinking about it – as anyone present who has ever written a word will understand. The more I thought the less I knew – does it ever happen any other way?

Yesterday I might have been inclined to say *yes*, there is a fence between adult and children's literature, goats on one side of it and sheep on the other. Today I could as readily say there is no clear division, and the goats and the sheep, according to one's inclination or perception, are varyingly interbred.

This does not mean I lack the courage of my convictions, it is simply that I have no inflexible feelings about it and am prepared to *accept* what turns up. There are times in life, as now, when one has inflexible feelings about very little; to hold a conviction does not necessarily mean you are right, you may simply be ignorant or stubborn or stupid. And not to hold a conviction does not necessarily mean you are apathetic or lost or gutless; it may indicate a return to the golden age of adventure and discovery.

I am not a politician, thank heaven. Kissing the babies isn't so bad, but that Straight Jack – Forthright Sam image is too

94

much for an honest man to live with. Constitutionally, like my children after me, I buck at following a set course, prescribed by myself or charted by others, and go all peculiar if expected to hold to opinions expressed last week or last year. At heart, down where the real man lives, I think most of us are the same.

One must be able to change one's mind, one must be able to argue with oneself, even publicly; one must be able to grow; one must be free to turn off, to tune out, and come in for a new adventure along a new road. In a hundred years you'll be dead. It'll be too late then. Why die before your heart stops and they decide it is expedient to put you in the ground?

Who discovers a book to write or an idea to express or an adventure to live if he locks the door and stays inside? Never to take the key out, is something I have learnt. Leave it there, for yourself, ready to turn. Leave it there for someone else to come inside.

How boring to be told you said green was blue in 1952 and if you do not continue unequivocally to support the view, you are, politically or intellectually or artistically or morally, a double-dealing damask dinner napkin or something of the kind. This can only be death or despair to a free soul. Worse still, to be held to an opinion expressed by some other member of the same team, the same political party, the same creed or the same breed, whether or not it expresses a majority ruling. The majority need not be you and there is no reason why it should be. What is a majority anyway? Everybody sheltering in everybody's shade.

I remember saying some months ago that I do not regard writing for children as a minor or a special sub-division of literature. This was not a *blunt* definition. I went on to say that when I address myself to children's literature I address myself to literature, and when as a writer I address myself to children I address myself to equals, and knew of no valid reason why I should adopt any other attitude. From my viewpoint, then and now, if a writer's motives are less he is playing around.

It is sometimes said that this particular book for children or

95

that particular book for children, of outstanding stature, has been achieved by accident, or was all a bit of a joke when the writer set it down. There are shades of meaning, I know, but generally I do not believe this. Admission to accident or joke is the modesty of the writer, or his reluctance, for some other reason, to own up to what went on. That book and that writer and that kid engrossed are equals, are there together, sharing an experience in literature, not literature scaled down or in miniature, an experience in literature, an extremely difficult experience to conceive and create and sustain.

I see no conflict of definition in this idea, however grandiloquent it might appear to be to people who go on regarding creative work for children, other than the hallowed classics, as unworthy of appreciative discussion. This narrow and destructive attitude is difficult to bury, though every now and then, from some faint encouragement, we brightly ask, have the knockers finally dug themselves a grave?

Good writing for children is obviously part of literature as a whole, just as good writing for anyone else is obviously part of literature as a whole. If you plant a rose, you grow a rose. If you plant a vine, a vine will grow. Their roots are in the same earth; their branches are in the same light. Who is to say, in ultimate terms, that the one or the other will bring the greater joy? Or the lesser? For any one man or any thousand men. And who has the wisdom to predict this, even for himself – or the right to speak for all? To me, this is self-evident and to have to express it is tiresome and faintly embarrassing, yet, by their utterances at almost every literary occasion I hear about, speakers, who should be much better informed, reveal their own ignorance and reinforce the ignorance of others by continuing to allude – if mention is made at all – to books for children and their writers with careless and condescending inaccuracy. That is about as nicely as I can put it! Are the achievements of so-called adult writers dismissed as inconsequential because bookstands creak beneath the weight of rubbish produced by their less committed colleagues? Does one demote sculpture in general to the shudder league because garden shops sell a million concrete gnomes with red concrete hats on? Is the child in the corner with a book, a nothing?

There are times of tiredness and frustration when I ask myself why is it that writers for children, particularly, have to go on, year in and year out, expending their creative and nervous energies preaching on public platforms, both to the converted and unconverted, when they should be at home and would much rather be at home, at peace, at their desks, producing? Two arduous years have gone since I completed my last new story; there are reasons for this, but not the least is the recurring need, the obligation I have heard it called, to grope off to yet another aeroplane, to go through the whole blamed thing yet another time, to defend or proclaim the cause somewhere in the world.

Why is it so? Why do people have to be told? Is it because of uncertainties, of memories of what we read ourselves a generation back or more? Troubled memories of lack of substance and style, of lashings of racism and imperialism and class indoctrination and absurd moralities, with, Heaven help me, titles like *Meet Simon Black* or *Simon Black in Peril* written by Southall in his adolescence thirty-five years ago? But in fairness to honoured names, they were not all *that* bad.

Is it because the books we buy now to give to "undiscerning innocents" are pretty poor stuff tailored to fit a price we are prepared to pay? You've taken a peek inside, perhaps, and shaken your head a while.

Is it because we associate children's literature with books called *Bertie Bear's Birthday* or *Nurse Neilson to the Rescue Again* in some mass-production format like packets of detergent or service-station give-aways, and must often be reassured that the millions of dollars going into libraries for children, and into the training of specialist librarians and teachers, and into salaries and awards and subsidies and bookstocks and associated services, are not part of a gigantic swindle chargeable to the consumer and the taxpayer?

Is it because we prefer to be told about children's books rather than make the effort to learn for ourselves from an intelligent sampling?

Is it because we bring to books for children, even to good books for children, unreal and unsympathetic measures to judge by?

No good coming to a book about people in a bushfire thinking, "Good God, not another: I couldn't stand one more," when that book is written probably with very special insight for kids who are meeting up with a bushfire situation in literature for the first time. Nor does it become you to say, "Aha, I knew it, saved on the last page by rain", when in real life that is what has happened so often. Ask someone who knows. Ask someone who has been saved by rain from an overwhelming conflagration in the classical "nick of time". Ask me.

No good coming to a book about a few kids fighting to survive without help from parents or grown-up friends with the attitude of mind that says, "The theme's been done to death, by Southall for one; there's nothing more about it anyone can say." Read the book and see. Read it through with a kid's eyes if you can, yet read it as an adult just the same. Remember that this experience, for some, will be new; will be giving dimension and life to a situation a child might have imagined for himself with excitement or nervousness or fear. Spare more than a moment trying to recall the *real* kid you were at ten or twelve or fourteen, just as the writer has had to do; an exercise in re-living or refreshment or rejuvenation that cannot happen in a moment; it is not an easy feat of recall.

Pick up anything determined to be bored, and you will make your point handsomely. Pick up *War and Peace* with that determination and you will not last to page 19.

Are there any new themes? Are there any experiences not already explored? Millions of storytellers hard at it for thousands of years. Bound to be some overlapping of material here and there. Plot-outlines sketched in a few words resemble others pretty closely, I hear. The variation is in the telling – not in the sixty words of blurb outside – in the sixty thousand words that start inside.

No good coming to a book for kids about love, all brassed off by a surfeit of adult sex, expecting to be titillated, when the sublieties and delicacies of the mood the writer is exploring are very finely tuned. Conversely, no good coming to the same book with emotions diluted or inhibited by the repressions and sentimentalities of another kind of childhood in another kind of age. And not much sense horning in, either, all bull-headed and holy, looking for bits to be publicly outraged about – they're easily found if you want to find them. If you have difficulty sighting them clearly, make them up for yourself.

As I see it – and I speak only for myself now – writing for children is a special activity dependent upon special insights and sensitivities. It is not for everyone, the capacity to do it, *or* the capacity to appreciate the end-result. Perhaps one is born with the aptitude, with the leaning that way. Perhaps it happens. Perhaps you wake up one morning and it's there. I have a recollection that that is the way it might have been. One morning, with twenty-five or twenty-six books of other kinds behind me, a completely new world was suddenly there; the world for me that began with a book called *Hills End*. Because of *Hills End* and what came after it, I stand here.

Story-telling, as I see it, is a recreating of life, a breathing of life into plausible characters and of facing honestly every naturally occurring situation those characters meet. In other places at other times I have endeavoured to describe how creating a story happens to me, and why creating a story happens to me. This, apparently, is of interest to people, though, to the writer himself, it is as commonplace as breath. To put in a few words the substance of an hour-long lecture of a year ago, I would say that the writing process for me is a voyage of discovery into the day-long surprises of the imagination, and that I undertake the journey because I am drawn to the excitement of the discovery. The process may differ with other writers – it may not be the thing for them, but it is the thing for me. So it

99

happens for me my way. Because I'm me. Not because I write for kids. If I could be bothered to write for adults I would not change, I would not suddenly put on my best clothes, I would function in exactly the same way, using the same garments. The intention would be different, that's all. And the result would be different.

I am held to books for children at this period of my life because the keen and inquiring mind of the healthy child does something to me; and the capacity of the healthy child to be moved to wonder and excitement over simple things does something to me; and the delight of the healthy child in his body and its awakening powers does something to me; and the fear and bewilderment and truculence and timidity and courage and cowardice and goodness of almost every kid who ever lived absorbs me. Perhaps I am a case of arrested development. Perhaps I find the innocence and conflict of childhood more in tune with what I am. Perhaps I am a sensualist and have learnt that first encounters are miraculous, and that all childhood is a first encounter and miraculous.

I have spoken at another time of one of the most common criticisms levelled against writers like me – that we write about children and not for them. I regard this empty-headed cliché as rather silly, as a careless rattle of the word-juggler's barrel. I never write for children except that the child I was rises to a position of some command – his viewpoint of the world is there to direct me; and children I know now contribute significantly, not actively by doing anything for me, but by their existence, by my awareness of them.

If Mary aged ten can't understand me, and Jonathan aged fourteen is bored stiff, and Mary and Jonathan can be multiplied by ten thousand in this city alone, I am not going to collapse in a heap about it – it is simply that Mary and Jonathan cannot tune into me. There is no compulsion. Why should anyone expect them to tune into me if they don't want to? But Helen aged eleven and Paul aged thirteen *can* tune in. It's a matter of preference, of taste, a personal thing. "It's not a book for children," I have heard people say. "I gave it to our Hugh and he couldn't make head or tail of it." What an incredible leap from a standing start. What an assumption. Worse still, to read it in the course of a review!

No one expects every adult in the world to enjoy Patrick White or Thea Astley or John Updike, thousands can't abide them, but does that make White or Astley or Updike into smaller quantities, does it make them into writers of no appeal to adult taste? Should Leon Garfield or Patricia Wrightson or Ivan Southall or writers like them be considered off track or out of touch if a million kids can't stomach what they write? Negative responses have nothing to do with the case. And often so-called expert adult opinion has less to do with it. The world is full of psychologists, amateurs and professionals, testing their theories, drumming up new ones. Yet it is true that the finished book belongs to the reader to accept or reject – the finished novel for children or the finished novel for adults, I see no difference.

If, for any reason, the age of readership to which the book should appeal is in doubt, leave that decision to others also. Neither the author, nor anyone else, should worry too much about it. Leave it to the book, if you like: a good book is not a dead thing, it can solve some issues for itself. If it is right for ten-year-olds, it will make its way to them. If it is right for grown-ups, it will find them eventually. If it is right for fourteen-year-olds, it will get to them. If it is right for its own kind of people, no matter how old or how young, little by little it will travel its journey, perhaps straining the author's patience or travelling along quietly years after he has lost specific interest.

When a manuscript becomes a printed book the author should seriously consider stepping aside and leaving the celebrations to others. It is difficult to defend a book, or justify it, or explain it, if you are the author. A serious work of fiction has its own personality, its own morality, its own soul, and the writer has passed through an experience gathering from it all that he can whether it always reflects his own soul or not. Thus a book has its own existence and goes its own way, lives its own life, and like any other human thing presents a different face to every person who encounters it. How can the author cope with this? The book has gone from his life and his control. He may have moved far away from it or far ahead of it and makes a mistake, I think, if he offers himself for cross-examination. Even on a public platform he should state, categorically, no.

A book is a creation of mood, the better the book the more complex or delicate the mood. You cannot turn that mood on again, easily, completely, coherently, *on demand*. You might never turn it on again as long as you live. I have tried to answer searching questions at different times but cannot be sure I have managed to give an honest answer. The mood, and the answers to fit it, went away from me when the book passed out of my control. Nor can I measure or predict or promise the relevance of a book to any reader – this is a matter of agreement or disagreement between the reader and the book and the mood of the hour in which they meet.

I asked that I might be free to argue with myself, but I appear not to be arguing. It seems to me I am repeating a basic feeling over and over again and see no need to take it further. I am convinced, as much as I can allow myself to be convinced about anything. I know the answer to the question as it relates to me at present. I am not responsible for the answer as it relates to anyone else and would not dream of expecting anyone else to accept my opinion as anything other than my opinion.

My answer is *yes* – there is a boundary between children's literature and adult literature, a boundary of magic and wonder and simplicity in the mind and heart of the writer as he puts it down. And my answer is *no* – there is no boundary between children's literature and adult literature; each, for the right reader at the right time, is part of the whole.